ROUTLEDGE LIBRARY EDITIONS: PSYCHOANALYSIS

Volume 2

THE PSYCHO-ANALYSIS OF THE NURSERY

THE PSYCHO-ANALYSIS OF THE NURSERY

ALICE BALINT

Routledge
Taylor & Francis Group

LONDON AND NEW YORK

First published in England in 1953 by Routledge & Kegan Paul Ltd

This edition first published in 2016
by Routledge
2 Park Square, Milton Park, Abingdon, Oxon OX14 4RN

and by Routledge
711 Third Avenue, New York, NY 10017

Routledge is an imprint of the Taylor & Francis Group, an informa business

© 1953 Alice Balint

All rights reserved. No part of this book may be reprinted or reproduced or utilised in any form or by any electronic, mechanical, or other means, now known or hereafter invented, including photocopying and recording, or in any information storage or retrieval system, without permission in writing from the publishers.

Trademark notice: Product or corporate names may be trademarks or registered trademarks, and are used only for identification and explanation without intent to infringe.

British Library Cataloguing in Publication Data
A catalogue record for this book is available from the British Library

ISBN: 978-1-138-93453-5 (Set)
ISBN: 978-1-315-65239-9 (Set) (ebk)
ISBN: 978-1-138-94315-5 (Volume 2) (hbk)
ISBN: 978-1-138-94316-2 (Volume 2) (pbk)
ISBN: 978-1-315-67269-4 (Volume 2) (ebk)

Publisher's Note
The publisher has gone to great lengths to ensure the quality of this reprint but points out that some imperfections in the original copies may be apparent.

Disclaimer
The publisher has made every effort to trace copyright holders and would welcome correspondence from those they have been unable to trace.

THE PSYCHO-ANALYSIS
OF
THE NURSERY

by
ALICE BALINT

ROUTLEDGE & KEGAN PAUL LTD
Broadway House, 68-74 Carter Lane
London

*First published in England 1953
by Routledge & Kegan Paul Ltd
Broadway House, 68-74 Carter Lane
London E.C. 4
Printed in Great Britain
by T. & A. Constable Ltd
Edinburgh*

PREFACE

THE English publication in 1953 of this book, which was originally printed in Hungarian in 1931, calls for an explanation. The more so as it was quickly translated into German in 1932, French in 1937 and Spanish in 1939.

The reason is that soon after the appearance of the German version, by the author herself, we received a letter from an assistant master of a small public school asking for permission to translate the book into English. Although his work was done with great care and enthusiasm it proved to be unacceptable. Years later the headmistress of an approved school, an English scholar, prepared another translation prompted again by admiration for the ideas expressed in the book. This version, although better, was still inadequate, but it was used as a basis by Mr. James Strachey who translated one chapter of the book, the fourth, which subsequently was printed in the International Journal of Psycho-Analysis in 1943.

In 1939 we moved to England, and soon realized the very great difficulties inherent in expressing in English experiences

PREFACE

and sentiments of continental nurseries. My wife was planning to prepare a translation herself when she died suddenly at the beginning of the war.

Here the matter rested till our son, educated first in Hungary and then in England, became a qualified doctor and while serving in the R.A.F. translated his mother's book from the original Hungarian, with the help of his English wife, another doctor.

I am greatly indebted to Mr. James Strachey for permitting me to use his translation of Chapter Four, to Miss Nancy Procter-Gregg who, using my son's rough translation, practically rewrote all the other parts.

MICHAEL BALINT

CONTENTS

PREFACE
page v

INTRODUCTION: NURSERY AND GROWN-UPS
page 1

I. THE EDUCATION OF INSTINCTS
page 11

II. THE ŒDIPUS COMPLEX
page 32

III. THE CASTRATION COMPLEX
page 62

**IV. IDENTIFICATION:
THE CONQUEST OF THE EXTERNAL WORLD**
page 92

THE CHILD AND HIS EDUCATORS
page 107

CONCLUSION: THE CHILD'S LIBERATION
page 128

APPENDIX: FUNDAMENTALS OF OUR EDUCATION
page 140

INDEX
page 147

Introduction

NURSERY AND GROWN-UPS

IN civilized societies, the nursery is one of the most mysterious things. It has its own language, its special customs, and its quite particular problems. And this is not surprising. The nursery is, in fact, the place where prehistory and civilization meet. There, day by day, the miracle of the transformation of primitive into civilized man is being enacted.

But it is less readily understandable that the children as well as the grown-ups concerned surround nursery doings with an element of concealment, and tend to forget about them as soon as possible. It is like the *parvenu* who thrusts into oblivion the days when he was uncertain about knives and forks. The comparison, indeed, goes even further, for just as successful social climbers like it to be thought that they have always belonged among the upper classes, everyone likes to think that even in the cradle he was a civilized being. Herein, perhaps, lies the psychological reason why men began to be interested in what cultural aptitudes could have been inherited from their ancestors much earlier than in the question of how they themselves have developed; in other words, why the theory of heredity preceded psychology. Once it is certain that cultural qualities are present in us from the first, we can the more easily gloss over that brief transitional period when we were all savages. But in the history of Darwinism we have a good example of the influence that feelings, in this case vanity, exert in the development of science.

So it comes about, that although most people in fact play the two parts in the nursery, first as children and then as educators, there is hardly anything so difficult to discuss as this enigmatic world within a world.

This emotional factor largely accounts for the fact that psycho-analysis only arrived at reliable data about childhood by a roundabout way, although from the first Freud had naturally been looking for the most hidden psychological motivations. The first enlightenment came, not from the nursery, but from adult neurotics, whose analyses established that the origin of their ailment was closely related to happenings in their earliest childhood. This fact, remarkable enough in itself, appeared the more extraordinary in that the sufferers themselves had no memory, until their treatment, of those events, so important for them, or at any rate had no suspicion of their significance. In the light of this evidence Freud formulated the concept of *repression*, a method of defence against the retention in consciousness of certain distressing experiences. This led him to turn with ever-increasing interest to the mental life of early years. And here he made another, and no less surprising, discovery. There is no significant difference between the childhood of the healthy and that of the unsound, that is to say, we all go through the same development, and partially settle its conflicts by the same expedient of repression, as do patients. The essential difference between sickness and health in this field lies simply in the intensity of the conflicts, and their aggravation derives usually not from inner disposition but from external shock—the 'trauma'.

With the discovery of repression fresh light was thrown on another common human characteristic, to which no one before Freud had paid much attention: normal adults very rarely remember the first four or five years of their lives. It was generally considered that this lacuna was to be accounted for by the elementary nature of infantile intelligence. This hypothesis was supported by the fact that such few shreds of remembrance as we do retain from early childhood mostly concern things of no particular meaning, coherence, or interest. When we are grown up, we find this selection of memories inexplicable. Decisive events pass over our childhood consciousness without apparently leaving any trace in our minds, while single insignificant impressions stay with us indelibly for a lifetime.

This general view seems to have much weight on its side, but the awkward fact is, that children's behaviour runs entirely counter to it. The normal infant is curious, alert, anxious for knowledge. Its direct remarks, its overflowing feelings, all demonstrate the richness of its mental life. It is 'impudent'—it wants a part in everything. It is an *'enfant terrible'*—noticing and remarking on everything. It is suspicious and critical—it can judge by the event. So, undeveloped intelligence can hardly be the ground for our only retaining stray shreds of memory from what is perhaps the richest and most eventful period of our lives. Today we know that this considerable deficiency of memory, extending over several years, is to be ascribed to repression. And we know too what kind of events they are that cause the whole of early childhood to become the object of repression.

Repression is a very important factor in the attitude of grown-ups towards the nursery. Repression of *one's own* memories of childhood constitutes the greatest obstacle to learning to know children as they really are. We do not want to see in our children the things we managed to obliterate from our own consciousness, and if they do force themselves on our attention we can only see them as abominations which ought to be eradicated. In the world of the Christian priest the radiant gods of Olympus are changed into fiends, and childish manifestations of instinct, which fall victim to the process of education and civilization (are in fact repressed), appear to us sinful and wicked.

This applies above all to the sexual instinct, which, as psycho-analysis has demonstrated, does not emerge in one's life for the first time at puberty, but is present in all individuals, normal or abnormal, from the moment of birth, and manifests itself in a great variety of forms. Freud in his work on childhood sexuality said that it was really shameful to have had to 'discover' that it existed, since every person with sight and hearing can observe its manifestations. It is, however, a fact that the description of just these manifestations gave rise to the greatest contradiction. People were able to stand the idea that in certain abnormal cases signs of sexuality in early years might be possible, but they were shocked and repelled by the notion that this same theory applied to everyone alike. It was felt to be profane that anyone should counter the conception of the tiny child as an innocent angel, and it was not realized that Freud himself, when he advanced this theory, had long got away from seeing childish expressions of instinct as either sinful or shocking.

Thus comes the paradox, that those very people are most ready to be horrified over children's depravity who most hotly maintain the notion of the purity of childhood. We have all heard jokes in which the child who knows it all shows up the adult to his disadvantage; but the emancipation from repression, brought about by the joke, is only momentary, and grown-ups, although they laugh, do not take in the fact that at the moment of seeing the joke they are actually confronted by the truth.

And yet, if sincerity could be made compulsory, it would be apparent that much is really known of the child's true nature, although this knowledge is only accessible under strictly determined conditions. The jokes just referred to are an indication of this, but it is especially obvious in the case of those concerned with the upbringing of small children, that they know much more while they are actually in the nursery than after they come out and shut the door behind them. It is a familiar fact that in early womanhood girls often recoil from the nursery atmosphere, yet swing over entirely to the opposite attitude when they themselves become mothers. It is commonly said that this is their sacrifice to mother-love. But I am of the opinion that the change is to be accounted for by the fact that in the relationship between mother and child feelings and activities are permissible which propriety otherwise forbids. In the nursery we can—to take one example out of many—indulge without blame the instinctual wishes to see and touch the sexual organs, and the naked body generally, or to observe the various bodily functions. In this lies the deeper meaning of the commonplace saying that through our children we renew our own childhood. When bachelors are facetious at the expense of fathers who handle the pot, there is a large ingredient of unconscious jealousy; the one is bound to feel disgust where the other may let himself feel pleasure. Yet even parents themselves can only give themselves over to these infantile gratifications within certain limits. We can notice that mothers and nurses will discuss freely amongst themselves the children's affairs, their caresses and their naughtiness, but do not like to do so before strangers or even the men of the family. It is as though they had a guilty feeling over having shared in the primitive pleasures enjoyed by the infants in their charge.

A similar reserve is shown regarding much of the vocabulary of the nursery. Words habitually and necessarily used in the course of nursery training fall under the taboo of the adult code of propriety. Such words, so important and familiar at first and later so generally prohibited, carry great significance in every person's development. The prohibition strikes particularly at the words; it is a common saying that there are things which may certainly be done, but not mentioned. One of the most important consequences of education is that things are divided into two classes, those about which we may and may not talk. It is almost as if there were a tacit agreement amongst us to assume that what is not mentioned does not exist. Silence means much the same as obliteration. What we may not speak of, we may not think of. A striking example of such an inhibition on thinking, founded on the prohibitions of education, is afforded in the literature of child psychology itself. In William and Clara Stern's two-volume work on children's speech, published in 1922, based on carefully kept diaries, not one single expression bearing on the excretory functions is given. One cannot imagine a nursery in which these matters would not have to be talked about, if only for the sake of training in good habits. So, if in the Sterns' very comprehensive vocabulary such words are missing, it is surely on account of a strong mental inhibition which, in spite of their scientific conscientiousness in recording, has prevented entire objectivity.

To talk of nursery happenings is a particularly delicate matter. If we translate children's expressions into scientific language, we are justly open to the reproach that our descriptions have lost touch with real life. But if we let the child speak for itself, we break the rules of decorum. I have chosen the lesser—in my view—of the two evils in using the children's own sayings in the stories I give as examples. In doing this I appeal to the elasticity of repression. It was precisely in connection with the nursery that we were able to establish that repression is no once-for-all exclusion of what we do not want to know, but a persisting process which, in Freud's comparison, is like the activity of a censor, who varies his strictness according to circumstances. And since it is not my aim to make the nursery fit for the drawing-room by shrouding it in a scientific veil, but, on the contrary, to encourage grown-ups to be not only educators but sober and objective observers of their children, a relaxation of the censorship is called for.

Yet how can this be procured? The psycho-analyst well knows how difficult it is to modify people's outlook concerning this censorship. An essential condition for objective observation is that we suspend the customary ready-made opinions which we apply almost automatically to human activities. These opinions are a protection to parents from becoming children in the company of their children. Many grown-ups adopt, in the first moment of their contact with children, a defensive, educative attitude. They generally begin with some such question as 'Are you a good boy, or girl?', 'Have you worked hard at school?', or, with the smaller ones, 'Do you love your mother?', 'Can you say "how do you do?",' and so on. But as educators we are permitted a less drawing-room kind of talk with children, just as doctors and nurses must set aside the normal standards of decorum in the course of their duties.

Science must confer a similar freedom. Serious research workers have not shrunk from spending many weeks, indeed many months, with the inhabitants of the monkey-house just in order to gain knowledge of the mental life of monkeys. Surely if this sort of sacrifice can be made in the cause of knowledge, it is not too much to ask that a similar scientific excursion should be undertaken into the nursery. We must go so far as to try to regard as merely instinctual manifestations things which we are used to calling naughtinesses; to see behind bad behaviour, stupidity, and obstinacy the sensations, emotions, and often rational thought which make a child's whole behaviour pattern intelligible.

Every concession towards hushing-up only makes it more difficult to probe and understand the facts objectively. No one today attempts to deny that such understanding is of practical as well as theoretical importance. And it cannot be had without study of the subject. Just as colonial officials are now required to study the customs and beliefs of the natives in the territories they are to administer, even though it may be their task to alter them, so we hold it necessary for the educator to be versed as thoroughly as possible in perception of the thought and feeling of the child, so that his purpose may be attained with the minimum disturbance. And just as European culture has been enriched by many strands from others, so, perhaps, we too may learn from our children, and a profounder knowledge of the child's—or more correctly the human—psyche will influence not only the methods of education, but its aims as well.

Chapter One

THE EDUCATION OF INSTINCTS

THIS chapter should perhaps be sub-titled 'The relationship of psycho-analysis to education', or 'training'. For we can only discuss the education of instincts on the basis of a clear notion of the fundamental propositions of psycho-analysis in the matter of education. The phrase 'education of instincts' itself denotes a programme closely linked to these propositions.

Yet to undertake an examination of the relationship between psycho-analysis and pedagogics (in the sense of 'training' or 'upbringing') is no light matter. It is actually one of the most complex, and so far least resolved, questions in psycho-analysis. What psycho-analysis can at present offer to pedagogics is neither a ready-made answer nor a prescription for education, but a fresh formulation of the problems and a programme for work.

So I am bound to disappoint those who hope to get from psycho-analysis detailed and universally applicable guidance on correct methods of education. This is partly because of the comparatively short time in which those with psychoanalytical training have been able to study the subject of children's upbringing, but partly also because it is no purely psychological matter, but in the highest degree a question also of social requirements, independent of the educator. Our demands on the child, and the things for which it must be educated, are determined by forces outside individual influence. The individual must submit, more or less, to very varying educational aims and methods, according to his cultural and social surroundings. Nowadays more freedom is being afforded in this field, but in the last resort no one can entirely escape the educational and other patterns of his environment and circumstances. Rather, the very purpose of education must be to fashion the child into a person adaptable to his surroundings. In our society, for example, a child must be trained to cleanliness by the age of three at least, and ready for school at six. By four or five he must have developed the sense of guilt (in other words, morality) and notions of propriety. When all this is achieved, no one usually is concerned to enquire as to the inward transformation which the child has had to undergo, or, more exactly, by what expenditure of mental effort on its part the result has been attained. In general, only the exertions of the educator are considered —the exertions required to inculcate the fundamentals of 'natural morality' into the small being who is perhaps both obdurate and uncomprehending, and indeed who often struggles against them with all its might.

It is pertinent to ask why we take so little interest in the hard mental labour performed by the child, when we have

THE EDUCATION OF INSTINCTS

all once had to go through the process ourselves. Our attitudes to the aims of education give us the answer. For most adults (that is, people already 'educated') the requirements of society seem such a matter of course that they find it almost unnatural that even a very small child should know nothing of them. It is a general enough belief that morality is innate in man. I know parents who worry seriously over the wickedness or evil disposition of their children of three or four, if they so much as fail to tell the exact truth, or covet things which do not belong to them. For such parents the bringing up of their children involves a never-ending series of wounds to their parental pride, since they have always to be teaching their offspring things which, to their minds, are the natural endowment of all properly constituted persons. Grown-ups, as a whole, betray the same turn of mind as the early missionaries who were convinced that the 'poor naked savages' would be happy if given clothes, since modesty must be a general human characteristic. On this account they had to believe the refractory 'savages' to be simply possessed by the devil, and indeed many concluded that indigenous tribes were perhaps not really human at all.

In view of this way of regarding existing standards of morality and propriety as inborn, natural human qualities, it is not surprising that it was so long before the question of the efforts required of the child was even posed. The sick man is not asked whether or how he would like to be cured, and with as little enquiry we 'prune the shoots' of a child's nature whether it likes it or no. But if we regard social requirements as practical conventions arrived at in the course of civilized development, observance of which is as

THE EDUCATION OF INSTINCTS

much to the advantage of the individual as of society, education, too, appears in a different light. It is no longer a 'pruning', an 'eradication of bad trends', but a matter of *implanting* and *habituation*. And to learn, or become habituated to, something is undeniably a toil needing effort. Children must work and make sacrifices in order to become like grown-ups.

In saying this we have not of course dealt with the aims of this early education in themselves. It is still true that they are independent of individuals, and evolve on the basis of social laws. But we can now define the problem of education as finding the way in which the child may attain the current practical goal with the least possible stress (that is, most economically). This is, in fact, a real reversal of the old way of putting it. Our primary regard is not for the pains taken by the educator, but for those of the child; and by studying the mental processes taking place in the child we try to find the answer to the question why any given educational procedure has proved successful or not.

It is at this point that pedagogics merges fully into psychology.

In applying the principles of psycho-analysis to pedagogics our first aim is not to alter the aims of education, that is society itself, but to give some help to the child in its task of adaptation. This is the fundamental point in such an approach, and in this context psycho-analysis can point here and there to mistakes in education, and can give guidance as to the ways in which, by greater patience and less severe moral demands, by a less prejudiced and—especially in sexual matters—a more liberal attitude, one may lighten the

THE EDUCATION OF INSTINCTS

burden laid upon man by the renunciations required by society.[1]

These 'renunciations required by society' are closely linked with education, as we have already seen. The nature of the connection becomes particularly clear if we consider the difference between our own educational procedures and those of primitive peoples. Among most of the latter, small children are given much more freedom, i.e. fewer renunciations are required of them, than with us. 'You mustn't' is hardly heard at all by these fortunate children. And they are more gently treated too; blows and scoldings being almost unknown. This particularly holds for boys, whose 'manliness' might, it is thought, be impaired by severe punishments. The children, for the rest, are no worse than ours, but also no better. Travellers have commonly been surprised by the remarkable patience with which adults bear the excesses committed by their rascally offspring. (And this applies as much to the African Negro as to the Eskimo of the far North, so it is not a matter of race or climate.)

This leniency towards children in primitive societies lasts usually only until puberty, at which time they are admitted to the ranks of the grown-ups by a ceremony calculated deeply to impress them, and with more or less severe accompaniments of torture. Their time of freedom is over, for the adult

[1] A greater tolerance, and especially a greater freedom from prejudice in the face of the primitive childish instincts, are just what we may hope for from the spread of psycho-analytic understanding. Its cultural mission is not therefore confined to mental therapy, but extends to the attempt to remove the very cause of neuroses by 'forming' men anew; thereby making itself superfluous as a therapy, though not as a psychology.

status carries heavy obligations. From now on the youth must observe the laws of the tribe and submit himself to the many and strict restraints which they impose.

Things begin to be very different when we come to the more highly civilized Mexican Indians. There, as we know from trustworthy accounts, children were subjected comparatively early to what we should call a strict education. The drawings of the Codex Mendoza show how children were forced to acquire the requisite knowledge with the aid of a variety of punishments, such as beatings, scoldings, kneelings, and standing in the corner.

It looks, therefore, as though the difference appearing in education is connected with the difference between the stages of civilization reached by a people. We can safely assume that more primitive peoples are not more gentle with their children than we because they love them better, or because they are by nature kinder. There is another factor at work, and we shall understand it better if we look more closely at the real meaning of the phrase 'everything allowed'.

The suckling is not kept to strict times and periods for his feeding; and weaning, too, is not taken strictly; infants who can already toddle may still have the breast when they want it. (This, incidentally, happens not seldom among country folk in Europe.) The little ones are not reproved for relieving their bodily needs where and when they like. And they can indulge in their genital sexuality just as freely. They masturbate under the eyes of the grown-ups, and try out coitus-like activities with each other, without bringing down on themselves a word of reproach. An eye-witness relates that an old Eskimo remarked on such a scene, with an indulgent smile, 'Well, children want such things too'. Naturally, in such circumstances children have ample opportunities to observe sexual life, birth, and death, whereby their desire to experiment becomes stronger.

In affairs of the mind, too, these children enjoy great freedom. An Eskimo father explained 'Children who are always being forbidden become stupid'. On this account children are allowed to be impertinent to their elders, and joke about their most sacred institutions. Rasmussen, one of the best authorities on the Eskimos, relates that he saw Eskimo children, to the great amusement of the elders, parody a religious ceremony which the latter carried out afterwards with great reverence and fervour. Asked what the spirits would say to such a thing, they answered in surprise 'But the spirits understand a joke!'

The American Indians permit their small children to affront their elders both in word and action. They treat these instances of rude behaviour as early signs of manliness, and are most careful not to intimidate their little ones by punishment or reproofs. An old Indian once remarked that he had never seen such a barbarity as a beating, except among the whites.

I think these examples show clearly enough the difference in approach between our upbringing of children and that of primitive peoples. It lies above all in the greater degree of freedom allowed to the instincts. Children in primitive societies may do and observe things which for our children might have serious results in mental trauma or in unacceptable behaviour.

Now comes the question, just what is it that has made a

so much deeper-reaching repression of primitive instincts necessary in our civilization? In other words, must a higher form of culture necessarily go hand in hand with early repression? To answer this question is to tackle the main problem of education. From the latter point of view it may be formulated thus: *Is the repression of instincts necessary for the maintenance of our civilization, and if so, to what extent?*

Later we shall see that even the children of primitive societies do not grow up without repression, and that they, just as much as our children, are obliged to renounce their strongest instinctual wishes. But we shall reserve closer consideration of this for the next chapter.

To be able to answer our question, we must first consider, *in what quarters of the mind is the work of education accomplished*, and what psychical resources are put at its disposal.

This proposition may sound rather theoretical, but we shall soon see that in fact it involves matters which are familiar in practice to all who have had occasion to acquire nursery experience. It is true that such experience is usually described, by those who have had it, as consisting of 'trifles' not worth discussing; yet I hope to be able to show the importance of these unregarded 'trifles'.

There are two main schools of thought as to the *educability* of children. According to the one, a child can be made into any kind of person we want, so long as we know how to do it; according to the other, an infant brings with it tendencies, aptitudes, and character traits which will develop, with time, in its individuality independently of its education.

Probably the truth lies here again between the two. We do not yet know exactly what features in an individuality are

THE EDUCATION OF INSTINCTS

inherited; but it is certain that every human being brings at birth a number of *instincts*, which down the ages have been inherited largely without modification. According to our present knowledge, these instincts are the given factors with which the educator has to reckon. As regards individual disposition, we have at present no better explanation than that it probably depends on the varying strength of the several instincts.

It behoves us, therefore, to form a clear notion of the *basic nature of instincts*. Their most essential characteristic is that —whether sexual or self-preservative—they strive for direct and immediate *satisfaction*.

Modern education opposes this basic characteristic in imposing regulations almost from the first day in an infant's life; the baby's desires are not fulfilled on the spot, but only according to a timetable (e.g. the set periods for feeds). Next, it proceeds to regulate other pleasurable activities according to grown-ups' wishes, as for instance in training to cleanliness. And eventually it requires of the child that certain gratifying activities should be renounced altogether.

We notice that education makes two kinds of demands on the child. First, to *tolerate postponement* of satisfaction, and second, in certain respects, full *renunciation*. And we must consider how the child, that impatient little instinctual being, can become conformable to these requirements.

Let us take the first kind. The infant has to become accustomed to bearing more or less severe tensions before it gets satisfaction. The most important result of this training is the moderation of the original tendencies that strive for immediate gratification into an adaptation to external

THE EDUCATION OF INSTINCTS

conditions and opposing circumstances. Every living being is forced towards this adaptation not merely by education but by reality itself. Painful consequences teach that immediate fulfilment may be more disagreeable than waiting—witness the old cautionary example of hot soup. And even the various instincts themselves may, owing to their original self-seeking tendencies, clash with each other; every mother knows, for example, how sometimes the suckling cannot choose between the nipple and its own thumb, or at later ages how the wish to keep a toy intact clashes with the longing to smash it.

Reality itself, external and internal, compels man towards mastery of his instincts, towards postponement, consideration, selection; thus, towards all manner of uncomfortable and unpleasant things which he learns to tolerate in order to avoid still more painful situations. In other words, the unconditional search for pleasure, the pleasure-principle itself, finally leads man to forego some gratification in order not to pay for it with greater pain. This is the essential teaching to be had from reality, which no one may evade with impunity, and which education proper can only emphasize.

The other demand, for *prohibition*, is a much deeper-reaching interference with primitive mental life, since it requires the child to renounce certain pleasures altogether. To this demand the small child, who cannot yet pass conscious judgment upon its wishes, responds with the repression of the forbidden desires. But the repression—as cannot be too strongly emphasized—does not dispose of the instinct behind the prohibited wish, but only prevents its manifestation in the original form.

THE EDUCATION OF INSTINCTS

Let us look more closely at the way in which the child reacts to the prohibitions and hindrances of its environment. We shall find that when a child is compelled to some renunciation, it tries in every way it knows to find a substitute. I once noticed a small boy who, when he had to put up with the slightest stress—had to wait for his meal, or his toys, or his father's return—would at once take to sucking his thumb. This pleasure, which he could give himself without help from outside, was his resort for consolation when his world proved unfriendly. A little girl whom I knew said, when I asked her why she sucked her thumb before going to sleep, 'because then I'm not alone'. A mother was trying to cure her daughter, aged two and a half, of the habit, and asked her why she really wanted her thumb; 'it's Mummy', was the answer.

These responses show us what makes these so-called 'bad habits' precious to children. For them, thumb-sucking is a grand device, making them independent of the caprice of the world around them. We shall return later to the question of why those in charge of education call these expedients 'bad habits'.

We may say, therefore, that two factors are fundamental in forming the man or woman—*the wish of the ego for unconditional gratification*, and *the resistance of the outside world*. Under their pressure man turns to the search for *substitute satisfactions*, and to the conscious use of them as a consolation mechanism. Broadly speaking, man is not capable of renunciation unless he can find some substitute gratification; but in this search he is forced, in the course of his development, to exercise ever greater ingenuity. Education takes account of this, and always offers some substitute for the renunciations demanded. Among such recompenses the most important, from the point of view of education, is the *love from the environment*, promised in effect as the child's reward for giving up its own way of obtaining pleasure.

Let us examine this in the light of a concrete example. One of the problems of greatest practical importance in bringing up little children is the training to cleanliness. I choose this example partly on this account, and also because it occurs at an age when the child is capable of expressing its wishes and feelings of distress unmistakably, while yet not so dominated by the influence of education that it dare not show its meaning openly before grown-ups.

Every mother knows that it is a pretty difficult matter to get a child into the way of relieving its needs at the times and in the proper place prescribed by its elders. When we look for the cause of this quite conscious resistance, we find that these functions afford the child a variety of pleasurable feelings, which are partly lost when they have to be performed according to the requirements of the adult world. It is important to remember that a child originally feels no disgust about its bodily products; on the contrary, it enjoys playing with them. It likes to touch them, admire them, smell them, even taste them; and besides this it is proud of its achievement, feels it has created something and prizes it as a valuable part of its own self. For example, children often look on it as a competition to see who can 'do most', or among boys who can make the biggest arc with his water. And the holding in of stool and urine is an amusement to them, and as the resultant stimulation increases so does the eventual pleasure obtained from evacuation.

Another reason for 'holding-in' is the primitive estimation, already mentioned, of the stool as a part of the self. I was told of a little girl, who for some time had suffered from constipation, and after a prolonged 'try' stood up and said, 'Mummy, I do mind so much'. 'What do you mind?' 'Giving my big job away'. The mother in this instance was understanding, and instead of scolding the child sympathized with her regrets; but she explained that the pain in her tummy came precisely from keeping the 'big job' inside herself. The result was a prompt and spontaneous evacuation.

Another small child, a boy of two, who was particularly recalcitrant over cleanliness training, on the occasions when he did do his 'big job' in the way the grown-ups approved performed a veritable triumphal dance, and insisted that all should admire his production. It was certainly no mere coincidence that this child, who held his stool in such esteem, should be one who found it very difficult to submit to regulation of this function. Note that he was well spanked if he had an 'accident', yet in spite of this deliberately preferred his own methods of relieving himself. Clearly, it was wounding to his self-esteem that his prized treasure should be treated as a waste product, to be disposed of as quickly as possible. His disobedience procured for him not only that he could do his task on his own and rejoice in it to his heart's content, but that his elders too had to show an enhanced interest in this important function.

Since in a 'well-conducted nursery' we try to deprive children of all these indulgences, compensatory gratifications must be found for them. They find one for themselves in the first place, when for example they treat other things as though they were their stool or urine, and play with them in the ways forbidden for these products; or they talk a lot about defaecating and micturating, set their dolls and animals on the pot, wipe and wash them, and so on.

Let us pause over this matter and consider more closely what is going on in the little one's mind. As we have said, the child has to renounce certain wishes, and achieves this with the aid of repression. Repression acts on an instinct much like a dam, or a river-dyke—that is, it turns it from its original course. Or we might put it that the instinct becomes homeless, and seeks new territory in which to settle. In this it is aided by another tendency, which serves the aim of finding pleasure and avoiding its opposite: this it is, which makes the child try to discover familiar and friendly things in the strange—and therefore at first alarming—surroundings of the outside world, by identifying the unknown with the known. In this way, to follow up our example, a small child's imagination makes urine of every fluid and faeces of every messy substance.

Here is an example: a boy of two was caught by his mother joyfully squeezing a tube of toothpaste into his mouth. He volunteered that 'I pressed it, and it made caca, and Eddie's eaten it'. The little boy had in a quite natural way identified the sausage-shaped mass, which came out with pressure, with faeces and as such he tasted it without any disgust.

Another two-year-old had been told about angels up in heaven, and on the next rainy day observed 'The angels are doing their wee-wee'. There, incidentally, he was spontaneously reproducing a legend which is widespread even today among primitive peoples.

A little girl of five entertained her friends with the following tale: 'There was once a Little Caca-Man, who jumped into the paint box and made a hole in the tube of paint and crept in, and when they wanted to paint and squeezed the tube it wasn't paint that came out, it was him'. This Little Caca-Man played other tricks too; he jumped for example into eggs and took the place of the yolk. It is clear that this little girl devised these tales as a compensation for the coprophilic pleasures she had to give up. This consolation is found by the aid of *identificatory thinking*.

It is noteworthy that the boy of two and the girl of five quite independently react by way of a similar fantasy to the tube from which a thick mass can be squeezed out. But we find differences, related to the difference of age. The two-year-old delights in tasting the toothpaste, in place of the forbidden faeces. The five-year-old, in contrast, more profoundly influenced by the prohibitions of training, retails the various pranks of a third party, the Little Caca-Man, and does not betray by a single word that she herself finds such things pleasant. Thus while the younger one openly avows the existence of the forbidden wish in himself, the elder denies all acquaintance with it and condemns its manifestations, although not very severely, as 'pranks'.

If, therefore, in the course of education, i.e. under the influence of prohibition, repression bars the way to direct gratification (as in the last example), this fanciful identifying also gives the objects concerned an enhanced significance as symbols or substitutes for the repressed ideas. By means of these equivalents, the original instinct can find another, *sublimated*, satisfaction. Making up stories, imitating education in play with dolls, playing with sand or plasticine, or painting, all afford such sublimations. A *robust instinctual disposition*, which has to seek satisfaction through a thousand by-ways, according to psycho-analytical findings augurs well for a life *rich in interests or talents*. Thus, when we discover powerful instincts in our children, we must realize that this is the material which, rightly directed, may turn to the best results.

But what is 'right directing'? We have said that the child reacts to external prohibitions with repression and a search for substitute gratifications. It achieves the latter either by gratifying another instinct or by diverting the one affected into another field. Education allows some of these efforts, and classes others as wrong and blocks them by fresh prohibitions. What guides this selection? We have mentioned thumb-sucking as a very general childish consolation; generally, grown-ups frown on this practice, call it a 'bad habit' to be got rid of, and combat it sometimes severely and sometimes more gently. Why? Thumb-sucking is a very useful device which helps children to bear life's disappointments. And yet, although without knowing why, the educators are doing the right thing for their purpose. We emphasized above that thumb-sucking is a method of gratification which tends to make the child *independent of its environment.* While contentedly sucking its thumb it has need of no one, and when it takes this refuge we have no means left to influence it. The passionate thumb-sucker may best be compared to the alcoholic, to whom drinking is so sure a shelter and so perfect a consolation that it takes the place of all else. If, then, this indulgence reaches a certain pitch, a child's accessibility to our influence becomes seriously threatened, and especially that most valuable part of it which depends upon the child's love for us.

But while we justify in this way the educator's attitude towards this primitive form of gratification, we must at the same time utter a warning against too stringent methods of enforcement. The primary thing to consider is, what are the grounds of a passionate addiction to this habit? First comes the matter of disposition, i.e. an especially strong pleasurable reaction to stimulus in the mouth (oral erotism),[1] and then that of certain traumatic events which the child encounters in connection with the mouth, e.g. abrupt weaning or other disturbances in the sucking period.

The best method of weaning from thumb-sucking (or rather, of preventing its becoming a passionate indulgence) is that we should offer as an alternate source of pleasure ourselves, in the stead of the small thumb. For example, when a child begins to suck its thumb we begin to amuse it until eventually it finds more pleasure in the game than the sucking. This naturally is especially the course to take when the thumb's consolation is sought for boredom or crossness, or for the distress of a broken toy; that is, when the child is trying by this means to evade the problems set by life. The

[1] Oral erotism is the term for the quality of mouth-activity which enables pleasurable sensations to be added to the merely nutritional functions. The same holds for anal and urethral erotism. Thus we note that in early childhood those parts of the body are the main vehicles of pleasurable excitation, which at the same time have an important biological function; and the stimulation of which, just on account of their biological function, is inevitable.

THE EDUCATION OF INSTINCTS

method is of course not applicable for a tired child who is used to going to sleep thumb in mouth; and here it is best to wait in patience. For the educator should never lose sight of the fact that thumb-sucking is a natural gratification for a child, quite suited to its age, and not a device adopted to annoy the grown-ups. The child is making a sacrifice when it abandons it, and it is our task to demonstrate that the sacrifice is worth its while. We have to convince it that—to stick to the example above—there is more joy in mending the broken toy than in peevishly abandoning the whole thing and sucking one's thumb. Whatever moderate pleasure, in spite of all this, remains in the habit we may safely tolerate, and if we have our children's love we can count on it that in time that, too, will be surmounted.

As a child gets older our auxiliaries in the struggle against this primitive instinctual gratification become more numerous. In the case of oral erotism particularly the position is eased by the fact that a great proportion of it passes over almost unchanged into normal adult indulgences. We have only to think of smoking, drinking, gourmandizing, and—not least—kissing.

We may summarize, therefore, by saying that the component primitive instincts may be satisfied in two ways: *independently of the outside world*, for example by thumb-sucking, retention of stool and urine—that is *egotistically*; or in such a way that the satisfaction creates a *relationship between child and environment*—that is, *socially*. The value attached to excrement is shown in a social way, in contrast to the egotistical 'holding back', when the child makes a present of its excreta to those it loves. On this basis the child comes to want to regulate the relief of its needs in accordance with the wishes of the grown-ups. As the folk-story has it, when the suckling passes water on its nurse's lap it 'pays for' the milk she has given. In one of the 'Contes Drolatiques' Balzac tells of an aged nun who suffered sorely from constipation, until one day she sighed 'Dear God, I make you a present of it'. Those who have the care of small children usually feel, very rightly, that this unpresentable 'present' is an expression of the child's love. A children's physician in Vienna told me how one day she made a morning visit to a little patient eighteen months old, and found him sitting beaming in his cot clutching a brown object in his hand. When she came up to him he proffered her a piece of hard faeces. Clearly he wanted, after his fashion, to repay the good lady doctor.

Interest in bodily functions brings a child nearer to the outside world in another way too. The fact that other people have the same needs greatly increases its interest in other people. One may observe how children of one and two years old, and even older, as a rule pay little attention to each other when brought together, but show great interest if one of them has to relieve itself. I myself have seen toddlers who were initially indifferent or even hostile towards each other become attracted over such a happening, and for the first time hug and kiss of their own accord without urging from their elders. Interest in the outside world is aroused even earlier in connection with oral erotism. We need not look further than the well-known infantile manifestation of putting everything into the mouth. The child's behaviour shows clearly that this is an attempt to get acquainted with the outer world. It is trying to get to love the objects it puts into

THE EDUCATION OF INSTINCTS

its mouth in the same way as, so far, it has only loved its mother's breast and its own thumb.

If we accept that the main aim of education is to form out of a child a social being, we must give preference to such methods of gratification as bring it closely into touch with its environment. However primitive the manifestations of its approach may be (putting things in its mouth, making gifts of excrement), we should value them as the first step on the road which leads to interest in people and things and to the ability to love them. In the course of development the individual has to give up these primitive attempts at *rapprochement* (like so many others), and must replace them by more advanced methods. But for carrying out this further renunciation the child is helped by just that psychical attachment which has been formed in the primitive way with the environment. When, that is, a child has once taken the first and most difficult step towards a love capable of sacrifice, it is comparatively easy to secure further progress in this direction.

Thus, a child's education originally relies not on its understanding but on its feelings. It is because of this that we so often notice that as soon as its emotional relationship with its environment is somehow disturbed, for example if the person for whose sake it became 'good' is absent, it relapses for a longer or shorter time into the original barbaric state. The Viennese physician I have mentioned told me how one of her patients, a little boy of two, already fully 'trained', lapsed into soiling his bed when his mother had some visitors to stay and could devote less time to him. In another case a little girl, also trained, wet her bed on a night when her

THE EDUCATION OF INSTINCTS

mother did not put her to bed as she was used to do. It is indeed a very common occurrence that a child will react with such relapses to a change of the person who looks after it.

We shall have occasion later on to consider the further development, wherein the original external demands become internal obligations.

We can now answer, at any rate partly, the question whether, and if so, how far, we ought to make our children resort to repression, in the sense of suppression of direct gratification of their instincts. *Instincts furnish the stuff for education*, and any education of instincts always means a *limitation of gratification*. From the instinctual aspect civilization is precisely a series of exactions, and it is evident that as civilization advances, so must the restrictions upon instinct. Instincts, indeed, still attain gratification in roundabout ways; but this is in fact a secondary process, although of the very greatest importance for the development of civilization. For it is the flexibility of instincts, *their variable aims*, manifested in creating ever new substitute gratifications, which made it possible for civilization to come into existence at all, and for us to support it.

Chapter Two

THE ŒDIPUS COMPLEX

WE pass now to the more dramatic side of nursery life.
So far, I have tried to show the way in which education can influence discharge of instinctual tension. From our present point of view, the aim of education is to direct instincts in such a way that they are diverted from the child's own person and turn towards the persons and objects of its environment. Training to cleanliness is an example, wherein the child's primitive pride in the excretory products of its body serves to make them valued presents, marks of distinction which it can confer on the people it loves. On this pattern the child's instincts are turned, both spontaneously and by education, towards the loved adults of its environment, so that eventually all its instinctual wishes cluster and crystallize about these figures.

The little child wants to find vent for all its instincts, as for instance the urge to see and fondle, in its parents. I know

THE ŒDIPUS COMPLEX

of a little boy of two who is at the height of happiness when his mother helps him with his 'big and little business', and if by chance his father is also present he announces with beaming face 'Daddy's watching me'. He rightly takes the managing of his clothes, and the attention paid to his performance, as evidence of love, and he lets us know in turn that he would gladly do the same for us. Children, who so readily show their nakedness, would like in turn to see the grown-ups naked; this is clear enough from their behaviour. They are very pleased if they can accompany grown-ups to the lavatory, bath-room, or dressing-room. Those toddlers who are denied all such opportunities show their interest just the same, by many signs; they listen outside and ask questions, and are pleased when they find the explanation for the grown-ups' mysterious temporary retirements. Not only erotism of defaecation, looking and touching, has a place here, however, but also genital erotism.

We know that genital erotism manifests itself even in babyhood, in infantile masturbation. Our babies, swathed as they are in nappies and shawls, yet soon discover the excitability of the genitals, and this in connection with the unavoidable stimulations occasioned by our care of their bodies. They soon begin to chuckle, or pay close attention, when their genitals are powdered and cleansed, and in time they try themselves to procure the same pleasurable sensations. We may conclude that from the very beginning the genitals have this property of affording sensuous pleasure. As is well known, unscrupulous nurses take advantage of this fact in soothing a crying baby.

Infantile masturbation should be regarded in the same

THE ŒDIPUS COMPLEX

way as, for example, thumb-sucking. At this age it has no more, but also no less, significance. It is a main characteristic of infantile sexuality that *the component sources of pleasure rank equal*; from the point of view of procuring pleasure, the genitals play no greater part than the other organs which contribute to this end, such as anus, urethra, mouth, and the skin generally.

At about the age of four or five, or indeed often even earlier, this state of things is altered and the genitals take a leading place. With little boys, the pleasurable sensations connected with urination promote this development. In the case of little girls things are much more complicated. Because of its hidden position the vagina plays hardly any part as a source of pleasure at this age, and on account of this the urethra and its immediately surrounding region, which assumes such importance in a little girl's masturbation, remains a dangerous rival to the genitals proper. I shall come to this matter in the next chapter, and meanwhile we need merely note that at this age sexuality becomes more unified from two points of view; firstly, from that of *object-choice*, since all a child's wishes become connected with its parents, and secondly from that of the whole *sexual organization*, since the genitals begin to play the leading part in the child's sexual life. Both these trends of development culminate in the phenomenon which, following Freud, we call the Œdipus complex.

Before we embark on a discussion of the Œdipus complex, I must again hark to the difficulties with which we have to contend in describing the psychical conflicts of childhood. For, as I must emphasize once more, we are dealing here

THE ŒDIPUS COMPLEX

with things which are in great part familiar to anyone who has the care of children, but which are seldom correctly evaluated. People often describe as amusing fancies or quaint imitation of grown-ups, incidents and problems that involve a child's deepest and most serious feelings. Such a faulty assessment of observed facts is a very common form of repression, and this being so, a discussion directed in fact against this repression will either meet with rejection or, what amounts to the same thing, be stigmatized as exaggerated.

This applies especially to our present subject. The Œdipus complex is considered, with justice, as the corner-stone of psycho-analytical theory, and upon it is concentrated much of the weight of opposition to psycho-analysis. In consequence people are apt to forget the important fact that the Œdipus complex is neither a dogma nor a theory to explain certain facts, but the *description and synthesis of generally observable and established facts.* The main fact here is, to put it briefly and bluntly, that at this early age *the object of love for the little boy is his mother, and for the little girl, her father.*

Consider the statement more closely. The child is in love with the parent of the opposite sex. How, in what form, is this love expressed? What is its aim, what does it seek to achieve? And what fate is it to meet? These are the three main questions that arise when we decide to take our statement seriously.

But to take it seriously is no easy matter, and, as everyone may see for himself, it gets more difficult the more we probe the details. The story of this love marks for all of us an important period of our lives, and we have all repressed our memories of it, because this story is one of a *hopeless love.*

THE ŒDIPUS COMPLEX

In saying this, I have anticipated something of which I must speak later. Before going further, let us examine the facts. Children, in the beginning, give full and open expression to their feelings. It rests with us whether we attach the right importance to these manifestations. I think that every mother of a son could tell stories of the declarations of love for her he made as a small child, and how he tried to be her cavalier and to deputize for his Daddy when he was away.

An eight-year-old boy said: 'Mummy, I wish I had two mouths so I could kiss both your hands at once'. A caretaker told me how, when she told her family that the landlord had been rude to her, her three-year-old son cried indignantly: 'Let him try that on when I'm about, I'll give him such a kick, I'll kick him out of his pants'.

A very small schoolboy, about to go away with his mother, assured his father most earnestly that he would look after his mother and also help her to manage the money, which of course was usually his father's affair.

Rasmussen, a children's psychologist who is not a psychoanalyst, relates in his *Psychology of the Child* how his daughter, aged five and a half, said one day to her mother: 'They say everyone has to get married. Is it true? . . . If you die, I'd like to have Daddy . . . but no, I'd sooner not marry'. 'Why not?' 'Because then one has to move, and that's so tiresome'.

Karl Abraham told the following story in one of his lectures in Berlin: A little girl of about four showed great interest in the question when her mother might be expected to die. Asked why this was such an urgent question for her,

THE ŒDIPUS COMPLEX

she replied 'Because then I'd marry Daddy, and I'd be Mummy, and I'd have lots of children'.

Another little girl of four reproached her mother, when she regretted leaving the countryside at the end of a holiday, with the words 'But Mummy, at home we have Daddy'. And I know of a baby girl of two and a half who cannot go to sleep at night unless her father comes to her bedside.

A boy of five said to his mother 'If I have a child, you'll be its mother and I its father'.

A boy of three saw his parents kissing, and said: 'Oh, do you love each other?' And his mother, who realized that jealousy was behind the question, answered 'Don't be upset, I love you too'.

A boy of six put matters surprisingly frankly. One day on returning from school he told the maid: 'You are my girl!' And when this was recounted to his father in the evening the little man, emboldened by the absence of reproof, said 'I've got a new girl since then'. 'Who?' 'Mummy'. Whereupon the father replied kindly but firmly: 'No, that won't do, Mummy is *my* girl, you get yourself another!' The child accepted this pronouncement with delight. (We shall come back later to this instance, which is interesting from the educational point of view.)

A boy of five, when his father was away for a while, gave vent to the speculation that 'Perhaps by now he is dead'. Asked by his mother why he should suppose this, the child replied 'Well, you know, he's such an old man'.

We can learn much from these stories. First of all, that the child, long before puberty, is, so to speak, already emotionally a grown man or woman. The little girl longing

THE ŒDIPUS COMPLEX

for her father and reproaching her mother for seeming to prefer the beauties of the countryside to his company, and the eight-year-old boy for whom one mouth is not enough to kiss his mother's hands, are excellent examples of tender love. The warlike son of the caretaker is a pattern of chivalry. And we can also note that the child not only loves but is jealous too, and knows very well who is its rival.

Yet these small lovers are here usually much worse off than are grown-ups in similar cases. They may be compared to people who have the misfortune to fall in love with the husband, or wife, of their best friend. For, indeed, a child is bound by love and tenderness to its rival as well.

Thus, even on the basis of this brief examination, we have found in childhood love the seeds of two serious conflicts.

First consider the one which arises from a child's relationship with its rival. Because of its love, it is in a situation where a person whom in fact it loves and venerates has to be regarded as an enemy. Why, however, must the boy think of his father, the girl of her mother, as an enemy, when either parent in fact allows—indeed requires—the child to love the other parent? Here we touch on the other conflict, for what is allowed and required of the child is not what the child longs for. This difference between what is allowed and what is desired is felt by the child as a *rejection*, and the grown-up rival, father or mother, is seen as the cause of it.

With this we have come to the darkest corner of the problem, which through repression is most vigorously debarred from coming into consciousness. For a child is not satisfied with being allowed merely to love; it demands

THE ŒDIPUS COMPLEX

everything; it truly wants the other person all for itself, and in the endeavour to possess encounters many real and actual difficulties. The nature of this 'everything' for which a child longs will be examined later. For the moment let us concern ourselves with the fact that the child—who has hardly passed the period of its instinctual life during which the demand is for unlimited, immediate, and complete gratification, and the reaction to the slightest hindrance is angry impatience—can only react with *hate* to the demand that it should share or renounce. The little girl who would like to be her father's wife suggests that her mother should hurry up and die, and the jealous little boy regards his father as being so old that his end may come any moment.

However hard a thing we find it, we must get used to the idea that our children do not only love us, but are also ready, if we get in their way, to get rid of us. This kind of love is plain enough in a child's attitude to its toys. Anyone can observe how a very small child will drop a toy no longer wanted at the moment—it is not put down, just dropped, and no notice taken of where it goes, unless indeed the crash affords a fresh amusement. It is the same with people who are a hindrance, or are unwanted by the child. And here let us not forget that children get their first unpleasant impressions, as well as the pleasant ones, from the figures closest to them in their environment—the parents. For this very reason the first emotional conflict is not that of the rivalry springing from love; the same sort of trouble arises much earlier in a child's life. We need only think of the rage aroused by attempts at training, or the grief of the nursling when its mother is absent, or consider that it is usually those in the closest relationship with a small child who have, where necessary, to deny its wishes.

A good illustration of the truth that a small child knows no compromise is the story of the three-year-old girl who coveted her godmother's bracelet, and asked if she might have it. She was told 'no', but that it would belong to her after her godmother's death. 'Then please die!', she said. Nothing happened, and a few minutes later she said reproachfully 'Well?' This little girl, for whom 'death' meant the same as 'not being there', in her longing for the bracelet demanded impatiently that her otherwise beloved godmother should cease to be, so that she could get her wish.

For a child, then, it is not impossible to feel alternating love and hate for the same person. As time goes on, however, these two feelings under the influence of education become incompatible. Then begins the psychical struggle which results in the repression of the one or other of them, usually the feelings of hate and hostility; this involves the repression at the same time of all the wishes connected with the feeling of rivalry which has caused the hate. This process is well and concisely illustrated in the example of Rasmussen's small daughter. The child first declares that after her mother's death she will marry her father. But afterwards she is frightened, obviously by the very violence of the death-wish towards her mother which underlies her plan, and she gives up the wishes just voiced, with the remark that it is tiresome and uncomfortable to get married.[1]

---

[1] On the pattern shown in this example, the result for the grown woman, in pathological cases, may be her complete rejection of normal sexuality.

THE ŒDIPUS COMPLEX

Having said this much, let us revert to the question of what is the aim of the love in childhood, termed the Œdipus complex. Here unfortunately illustration by anecdotes of children fails us in the task of elucidation.[1] This is partly because of the prudishness of adults, and partly owing to the effects of education, which by this age has already resulted in a considerable inhibition of a child's frankness and spontaneity. It is very rarely that a child of four to five communicates its thoughts so freely that it dares to express wishes of the kind in question; indeed, they seldom even find a place in the child's own mind. A further factor we must bear in mind is that the wishes arising here are such as cannot yet take concrete form because of a child's physical and mental immaturity. Probably a great part of this uncertainty is also a product of education. Be that as it may, the ignorance of our children certainly does not prevent their lively interest in sexual matters, but it does largely explain the various strange forms taken by childish love phantasies.

An example of children's invincible urge for knowledge in these matters is afforded by the following story—rather improper, but very true to life. A baby was expected, and before the confinement the elder little boy, to whom nothing was explained about it, was sent off to a relative on a farm. When the father was bringing him home again, the following dialogue ensued. The father: 'God has listened to our prayers and sent us a baby girl'. The boy asked several minor questions, then said suddenly 'Look Daddy, I know every-

---

[1] The knowledge we possess comes in great part from the analyses of both ill and healthy adults, and from psycho-analytical observations of children.

thing, but just tell me, did Mummy go to the bull or did they bring him to her?'

Children want to partake, somehow, in the pleasure which adults give each other. But what can this good thing be? Their guesses mostly concentrate round the fact, readily observable in most families, that the parents sleep together. The secrecy that surrounds the doings that take place in a bedroom enhances curiosity still further. Children have no doubt that what is kept so private from them must be something agreeable, and they imagine it on the pattern of pleasures known to them. In this way arise the typical infantile theories of married life which we meet in the analyses of healthy as well as sick persons. According to these childhood phantasies married intercourse consists, for example, in the parents relieving themselves in front of each other, or showing themselves to each other naked. An important and more legitimate rôle is played in these notions by the kiss, since it is the one activity of a sexual kind which even a child is allowed to know of. An important accompaniment of all these phantasies and musings is genital excitation, which dimly but definitely guides the child towards the reality. The voluptuous excitation of the genitals is a strong and irrefutable indication that this important part of the body must be concerned in the intercourse between the parents.

Let us not forget that a child's sexuality is stimulated by caresses, especially when, as so commonly happens, its parents take the child into their bed. In the course of these indulgences, regarded as innocent or in other words having nothing to do with sex, children try to find answers to the questions which haunt their imagination. They make discoveries about their parents' bodies, and they experience the pleasure that is caused by the physical proximity of a beloved being. I heard a mother, for example, recount how it was such a treat for her little son to be taken into her bed, so that even when he was eleven years old she still allowed it on special occasions such as birthday or Christmas. On the last occasion he surprised her by saying 'Mummy, you don't realize how I'm practically a man by now!' The mother was the more taken aback, as she had supposed her child such a 'little innocent' that he would not yet know the difference between boys and girls, although he had a little sister. We can imagine how strong the feelings must have been which prompted so shy a boy to so open a declaration.

The only defect of this illustration is that the child was not so very young; he was approaching puberty, the period when even common opinion admits that sexual excitation may be felt. Yet that same opinion usually rejects with indignation the idea that a boy might feel such stimulation in connection with his mother's person. We, however, go even further, and on the basis of psycho-analytical experience maintain that children of even three or four, or younger still, equally react with genital excitement to the pleasure caused by physical contact with the parents.

We have learnt from the analyses of both adults and children that the connection of genital excitement in childhood with certain particular persons has a crucial influence on the form of masturbation. By the third or fourth year of age masturbation is no longer a purely egotistical method of gratification, like thumb-sucking for instance, for it is allied

THE ŒDIPUS COMPLEX

with phantasies, concerned with wishes referring to the beloved persons—usually the parents. The *masturbation-phantasies* of childhood are among the *most deeply repressed contents of the mind,* and even at the moment of their formation they only rarely become fully conscious. As to the reason why those phantasies are so strictly censored, I will only mention at this stage that the main cause of the repression is the fear of retaliation for the hostile emotion felt towards rivals.

The content of these masturbation-phantasies of childhood is usually of a very simple kind. In the classical case described by Freud, 'Analysis of a Phobia in a Five-Year-Old Boy,'[1] the child while masturbating imagined his mother in a short vest which left her genitals visible. Thus, in phantasy, was fulfilled the child's wish to see the part of his mother's body which in reality he rarely caught a glimpse of.

Only when one has had experience of the evidence afforded by analysis can one estimate the enormous strength of the feelings which create these primitive phantasies. From analysis we learn what burning curiosity about the mysteries of sex torments children. It is no mere theoretical thirst for knowledge; children want to know about adult pleasures, so that they may be able to have them too. Like the six-year-old boy, for example, whose father said 'I won't take the boy to the pictures, to see a lot of love-films'. 'But Daddy, in that case how can I find out what love is?'

As already mentioned, genital excitation is the child's first clue to the solution of the secret. And it can learn other

---

[1] *Collected Papers,* Vol. III; Hogarth Press.

things from this too. When it occurs, impulses which surely belong to the heredity of mankind play their part. In a tiny boy arises a dark instinct to attack and overpower the one he loves. Probably this originates the sadistic conception, so common in children, of coitus and of love in general.

A boy just one and a half years old, seeing his parents kissing, said 'You mustn't hurt Mummy'. Yet, at the same time, he himself kissed his mother very readily, and even pinched her cheek and was obviously pleased when he saw that it hurt. The 'mustn't' was clearly applied only to his father, who was not to be allowed to kiss the mother—a right the little boy wanted to reserve to himself. This wish, too, in fact found expression, for he dismissed his father with the words 'Go and work!'

If children observe coitus, whether of animals or humans, they usually regard it as a fight. This notion does not exclude their recognition of the sexual nature of the act. They can experience for themselves, too, in connection with their games with each other, that fighting can induce sensual excitement. The same thing may result from playful scuffling with adults. Such games give great pleasure to both sides, but the same may sometimes also be said of more serious cuffs and blows, even those given in punishment. I heard a story of a little boy of four, whose mother (who often beat him) threatened once when he was particularly naughty to get his father to punish him; his answer was 'I'd rather it was you beat me, Mummy, I love you so much better'.

Childhood observations of coitus belong among those experiences of sex, big with consequences, which the parents themselves provide for their children almost always without

THE ŒDIPUS COMPLEX

being aware of the fact. When we point out what a child can perceive if it sleeps in their bedroom, parents usually answer that it sleeps soundly or that in any case it doesn't understand what happens. Only in retrospect, on the ground of memories elicited in adults for whom these observations made in childhood have so often been the starting-point for various conflicts, was psycho-analysis able to prove that children do indeed participate in the sexual excitement of the adults. Today however we can already see more clearly into these matters, and detect the indications which show that children, even if perhaps they do see or hear nothing, yet somehow sense what is going on. We have learnt, for example, in this connection to understand in certain cases a child's particular form of nocturnal behaviour.

I know of a four-year-old boy, whose father is only at home on one day in the week, i.e. for one night with his family; the child is particularly fretful and naughty on that day, will not go to sleep at night, and so on. A little girl of seven, who (like the little boy just mentioned) sleeps in the same room as her parents, wets her bed every night, except for the week when her mother has her period. To understand this instance we must recall that urination is one form of expression for childhood sexuality. Further, we must take account of the fact that for a little girl it is precisely the region of the urethra and clitoris that is the principal vehicle for sexual excitation, and that masturbation too finds its place here; and finally that urination is the familiar infantile method of outlet for every sort of excitement. The bedwetting in this case is a clear sign that the child is imitating her parents after her own fashion. The fact, which so surprised them, that it ceases during the mother's menstruation, strengthens our assumption. In another instance of a little girl, aged four, urination was again a sign of joyful excitement, so that when she saw her father arrive unexpectedly she immediately wetted for joy. The fact that even much younger children than these so often, by soiling their beds, disturb their parents just at the time of sexual intercourse is to be explained on the same lines.

This primitive form of the child's participation in the parents' state of stimulation is almost as though the child were wanting to mock the grown-ups: 'Look, I am asleep, I see nothing, I hear nothing, and yet I know all about it'.

This mocking rebellious feeling plays a rôle in the life of every child. In general, children are in reality condemned by the grown-ups to appear blind and deaf. In the time-honoured ostrich policy the grown-ups are satisfied that what children ought not to know ('a nice child doesn't ask about that') they will in fact not know. This pseudo-innocence, however, brings children to greater harm than the knowledge which we try to keep from them. For what they know, they dare not mention; what they want to know, they dare not ask about; all honest manifestation of their sexual life is regarded as something forbidden and reprehensible. In this way they come to acquire, right from the beginning of their lives, an attitude to sex that is distorted and unhealthy. They learn to consider everything that gives them this sort of pleasure as sinful, and mostly lose for life the ability to regard without prejudice the manifestations of the sexual instinct.

The harmful consequences of this mode of education are

THE ŒDIPUS COMPLEX

shown not only in the eventual attitude to sex, but also, and earlier, in the attitude of parents and children towards each other. We often find in the nursery a strange mixture of denial and admission, which dispenses with all honesty or true appreciation of things. The sexual morality outlined above, based on a lie, combines a complete denial of sexuality with full tacit admission of it in practice. On the basis of the fiction that children have no sexual feelings, grown-ups often allow themselves very far-reaching indulgences in that direction with children. Even direct playing with and caressing of the genitals is no rarity. Yet if the child betrays by mention or by question the feelings which such play arouses, it is thought to be naturally depraved, or it is supposed that some evil-minded person has put such things into its head. The child may see and hear, may in the form of caressing tenderness experience, anything and everything—because we put everything right by behaving (and getting our children also to behave) as though nothing has happened.

These 'innocent games' bind the child more closely to its parents and nurses than is desirable for its development. And, although such indulgences give a child great pleasure, they do not give it real happiness, for the dissimulation of their real nature awakens a feeling of guilt. From this it ensues that besides the erotic tie to the parents, felt as sinful and soon repressed, there arises a deep estrangement from them, not seldom bordering on hate.

On the basis of what we have said earlier, we know that because of the Œdipus complex a child's sexuality is tainted with a sense of guilt—on account, that is, of the hostile feelings towards the rival. Parents very often augment this sense of guilt, in that they, although themselves evoking voluptuous feelings in their children, call those very sensations wrong. The children therefore never quite know whether the grown-ups feel the same pleasure as they do, or whether it is merely a sign of their own wickedness. Adults' lack of honesty in relation to their own pleasurable sensations is one of the greatest obstacles to a true friendship between children and their parents.

Take, for example, the prohibition of masturbation. An enlightened mother, who does not want to scare her child unnecessarily, tells her ten-year-old daughter that she should give up this 'naughtiness' (i.e. masturbation), it is no more than a 'nasty habit'. Yet, the child must know from experience that this so-called 'nasty habit' is connected with very keen pleasure. What is she to think of her mother? Either she is an entirely different sort of being, who knows nothing of such feelings as the little girl has, or else she is a liar and calls an activity which she herself knows to hold something very enjoyable—a naughtiness.

Thus when, in time, a child learns to know the true feelings of grown-ups, it can no longer rejoice in their being identical with itself, but recognizes the treason and deceit that have been perpetrated. The parents lose the halo with which the children surrounded them at the time of the struggle for repression. Often, sexuality and respectability remain incompatible for life; so that children, when in turn they arrive at parenthood, equally cannot imagine that it is possible to retain their children's respect for their authority if they betray the fact that they themselves have a sex life. And so, from generation to generation, the same falsehood

THE ŒDIPUS COMPLEX

is perpetuated, although we all suffer from it in the same way.

In the case of the little boy who first selected the maid as his love, and then let fall that he really meant his mother, the parents behaved more boldly and frankly, in telling him that he must look for 'his girl' elsewhere. The father made just the right response to the boy's attitude. He took the child's feelings seriously, framing his refusal as though to a real competitor. In that way he augmented his son's self-respect, let him show his feelings unreproved, and at the same time showed him the way in which eventually he could find a consolation for himself. The conventional educational method here would have been simply to say 'little boys shouldn't talk like that', etc., and would have had precisely the opposite effect. The child would have been hurt in his love as well as in his self-esteem. And, since a rejection in this form would have reduced the stage of capacity for love which he had achieved to a lower one, a block would have been placed in the path which leads from the person of the mother to some other, permissible, object of craving. A further ill-consequence of such an attitude is, that in the child's unconscious mind it leads to an over-estimation of 'childishness', to the detriment of 'grown-upness'. In a crude schematization we may put it thus: the child's first attempt to be adult meets with complete failure; not only does he fail to achieve his end, but even the reality of his feelings is denied. Only if he contents himself with being a child can the boy have his mother for himself. Many neuroses are to be explained by the fact that the individuals concerned want to remain children, so that they may rejoice

THE ŒDIPUS COMPLEX

undisturbed in motherly care and love. In our example, in contrast, where the father does not pretend with the child, and unsparingly shows him the hopelessness of his present aspirations in love, manhood is at the same time made to appear as that beckoning age in which a boy will after all have the chance to fulfil his wishes.

We have already noted how great is the small child's curiosity about the mysteries of sex. One of its most striking manifestations is the question familiar in every nursery: 'Where do babies come from?' A trained children's nurse, with no psycho-analytical connections, once told me that in her first post, almost at the moment of her arrival, the five-year-old son of the family met her with the question 'You'll tell me truly, won't you, where children come from?' The little boy hoped that from this nurse, who seemed to have almost the qualifications of the doctor, he would at last get an honest answer. There was a baby of six months in the family, and probably this circumstance made the question so urgent for the elder brother. The parents took it for granted that the little boy, who from four had seen the visible progress of his mother's pregnancy, would think nothing of it all. Still less did they suppose that he had looked for a connection between the change in her shape and the arrival of the little brother. Thus it could come about that the child, whom the nurse described as much indulged, turned to a stranger with his burning problem, and had more trust in her than in his parents who were devoted to him. This is an illuminating example of how lonely a child can be in the most loving surroundings, if there is no understanding of what is going on in its mind.

THE ŒDIPUS COMPLEX

The problem of birth plays an important part in the life of every child. The question where babies come from is posed openly by most children sooner or later, and we all know that the small questioners are on such occasions usually swindled. This expression is perhaps too strong, but I must explain why I have used it. We have learnt from adult analyses, and in some favourable cases from little children themselves, that children feel that a fraud is being practised on them with the stork story and its variants. They watch from the window for the arrival of the stork who is supposed to be bringing the baby, or peer into the lake whence it is to be fetched, while a French child will search the cabbage patch, and an English one will investigate the gooseberry bushes. Incredulous, they ask if the stork brought the baby dressed or with nothing on, if it knew where to put it, if it rang the bell or could turn the door handle, and so on.

The Berlin caretaker's son, mentioned before, said to his mother when he was three: 'I know now that babies grow in women's tummies. Do you suppose I was so silly that I believed that I sat at the bottom of the Teltow Canal? Wouldn't I have caught cold? And how could the stork have brought me? Would he drop me down the chimney? I'd have got all dirty and hurt myself!' Only when he had learnt the real truth did this little boy betray how many doubts the parents' first answer had raised in his mind.

There is good ground for the persistence which children show over the problem of birth. The question where babies come from is a centre for a child's sexual interest. Freud pointed out in various of his writings that it arouses in the

THE ŒDIPUS COMPLEX

young minds the spirit of enquiry, and this is not surprising, for in this question the egotistical interest of a child comes into play, as well as the sexual. Very often it is the birth of a small brother or sister that makes the problem acute. Even with an only child the fear of the appearance of a rival is one of the most important reasons for posing the question. Jealous rivalry between children of the same family is never absent. For the moment I will not discuss the methods by which a child reconciles itself to the new situation. We are concerned here with the primary attitude to the new rival, which is, in essence, compounded of fear and hate.

A five-year-old boy, an only child, remarked one day, 'It would be silly of Mummy, wouldn't it, to want another child when she already has one?' A little girl of the same age, also an only child, when asked what she supposed children did when they belonged to the same family, replied promptly and concisely, 'They quarrel'. An old gentleman of seventy asked a boy of three whether he would like a little brother or sister, but added at once 'To this day I remember how angry I was with my little sister when she was born, although I was only just five at the time!' And a little girl of three, on being shown her new baby brother, said 'Perhaps we could exchange him in the shop for a penny balloon?'

It is by no means rare for this jealousy to be expressed in open hostility. One mother told me how her little son, usually a very docile child, was found by her one day, when he was two, preparing to smite his little sister on the head in her cot with a large piece of firewood. Another child, a little girl of three and a half, locked her baby brother into a drawer and threw the key out of the window. A little boy just

THE ŒDIPUS COMPLEX

under three expressed his disgust with his new-born brother in the following pregnant phrase: 'No teeth, red, and stinks'. (I owe this example to Karl Abraham.)

Such instances are endlessly available. The cause of the jealousy and rage is, naturally, the fact that the earlier favourite must now share the parents' love with the new arrival. In certain families, where a strict upbringing prevents the child from open expression of such 'wicked' feelings, one may often observe a radical transformation in its behaviour. From being docile and obedient it may become difficult and rebellious. Many children, formerly gay, turn quiet and sad after the arrival of another baby in the family and one often observes in them, temporarily at any rate, the signs of neurotic disturbance: waking in fright at night, anxieties, nervous vomiting, loss of appetite, and so on.

The second important driving motive in the interest taken in birth is the sexual one. From analyses and from unprejudiced observations of children made by others we have learnt that small children suppose that giving birth, like coitus, is something pleasurable, and they fashion their theories of it partly on the basis of what they can perceive, and partly on the indications given by their own instincts.

Rasmussen, the Danish children's psychologist already mentioned, has illustrated this point very instructively. His two little girls had a very free upbringing, as is evident from his book, *The Psychology of the Child*, which reports his observations. The elder, at about five, asked her mother 'Where is the baby that Aunty is going to have in the summer?' The mother answered, 'It is inside her tummy'.

THE ŒDIPUS COMPLEX

The child thought this very odd, and enquired after reflection 'Then did she eat it?' At the negative reply she embarked on further enquiry. 'Does it grow out of her flesh?' Again, no. Indefatigably, another question, 'Will it come out of her mouth?' The mother saw that she must supply the information, and finally said 'No, it comes out where she pees'. This frank enlightenment quite satisfied the small enquirer, who rounded it off for herself with the remark, 'Then she'll sit on the pot and then it'll come out and then it'll be wet and its feet will have to be dried'.

A boy of five, equally pleased when his mother gave him information about how he was born, said 'And then you thought you were going to do your "big job", and you pushed, but it wasn't your big job that came out, it was me'.

A little country girl of four happened to be present when an expectant mother began her labour pains. When the ensuing excitement and arrangements at last gave opportunity, the child asked, 'Mummy, tell me, is it her tummy or the stork?' Taken by surprise, the mother answered 'Her tummy', and the child said, 'Now there's only one thing I still don't understand, how you swallowed me'.

In these stories we may note specially how when the children ask about birth, they are also enquiring, although not directly, how the baby got into the mother's tummy. The simplest explanation occurring to most children is that the baby got into the tummy in the same way as food, and the fact that it, too, comes out below fits in very well with this notion. If, in Rasmussen's instance, the mother had not given so adequate an account, we may be sure that her daughter too would have evolved the general childish theory that the baby who can only get into the mother's tummy through her mouth comes out into the world through her anus.

This theory has for children the advantage not only of making the observed facts intelligible, but also of connecting the having of a baby with processes already long familiar and pleasurable. In the previous chapter I spoke of how the mouth and anus signify important sources of gratification for children. What more natural than that they should suppose that these two organs play an equally important part in the lives of grown-ups? Giving birth is imagined as a process like passing stool and similarly pleasurable.

The little boy, mentioned before, who asked the new nurse at once about his vexatious problem, used to spend the best part of his day in the lavatory, where he could sit for hours, musing. If we assume that he, who had had occasion to observe the change in his mother's shape during her pregnancy, also adhered to the theory outlined above, we can attach a meaning to his finding the lavatory such an attractive place. That must be the place for the miracle, somehow. But there, too, perhaps, arose the further problem and also the doubt as to the correctness of his own theory: what is the food from which a baby grows in a person's tummy, and where does one get it?

Children's keen interest and curiosity about birth show that they suspect that all sorts of attractions are connected with it. But it is only from analyses that we have discovered how ardently children wish for babies for themselves. Most people consider their games on this theme to be merely imitative, but on closer examination they reveal the hidden wish to be really like the grown-ups, to partake actually in the pleasures of giving birth.

Rasmussen's little daughter, for example, at five and a half years old, when lying one morning in her father's bed, tapped herself proudly on the chest and said, 'I have a baby in here . . . and when I am twenty, it will pop out'. Freud's case of 'Little Hans' shows how a five-year-old boy imagined himself sole progenitor of numerous children, whose every need he cared for, and to whom he gave birth in uninterrupted series in the lavatory.

Little girls' phantasies usually associate numerous babies with the idea of their future happiness. A child of four, the indulged only daughter of rich parents, told her grandmother: 'It's a lot of worry having fourteen children to wash and dress and feed, and' (she added with a sigh) 'all that without a husband'. But soon, she said, things would be better, for the chaffeur's son was going to marry her.

The great wish of a little girl of the same age, daughter of a landowner, was to be a plain farmer's wife with a lot of children. She pictured to herself how she would suckle and provide for the children, but of an evening sit on the bench outside the door mending her husband's trousers. She, also, had picked the small son of one of the farm-hands as her future husband.

The Berlin caretaker whom I have quoted before recounted how her daughter at thirteen would not hear a word on the subject of babies, but at three had scolded her mother for giving away some old clothes; her bitter reproach was 'But, Mummy, I could have used them for my children!'

THE ŒDIPUS COMPLEX

This description would be incomplete if we left out of account the rôle played by the father in children's phantasies about how babies originate. Our examples show that children suspect the connection between the parents' cohabitation and the arrival of babies. At the beginning of this chapter I mentioned the little girl of four who said that if her mother died she would be her father's wife, and then she would have many children. And in our last examples the little girls knew that husbands would be needed. The dream of a girl of six is interesting in this connection: she told it to her mother of her own accord, though with some embarrassment. She dreamt that she went to the dancing class with a boy she was very fond of, and she had on her best frock. Then she saw 'all at once, I don't know how, between us there was a baby in long clothes'. She was very happy with the baby and hugged and kissed it and loved it very much. (We may note that the child's circle was quite alien to psycho-analysis, so the telling of the dream shows how very important she herself felt it to be.)

Children, therefore, guess that somehow there must be a connection between the parents' living together and the birth of babies. A child of six began to worry his head about why, in fact, children resemble their parents. That they are like their mothers he found intelligible, since they grow inside them (this had been explained to him long before). But why should they be like their fathers? At first he tried to explain it to himself by the fact that they all lived together, but this theory soon had to be discarded, since the nannie lived with them too, and they didn't resemble her at all. Having got so far he finally had to come out with the direct question, what exactly has the father to do with having a baby?

In another instance the indiscreet questions put by a boy of five to a newly-married pair showed clearly that he already divined the connection between the intimacies of marriage, or rather between the secrets of a man and woman living together, and the arrival of babies.

I must add something very briefly on the question how much a child suspects of the rôle of the penis in conception. We note that the wish for a child is very closely bound up with the Œdipus wishes. It is thus a part of the child's sexual phantasies. We saw that spontaneous excitation or deliberate stimulation of the sexual organ (masturbation) accompanies these phantasies. This gives the instinctual foundation for that premonitory sureness with which children react correctly to the slightest indications in this direction. Naturally, here too there is no lack of strange phantasies; analyses have made us familiar with many remarkable theories as to the function of the male organ, which at this point I do not propose to consider in detail. I will only mention in broad outline two main types of such theories. In the first group are ideas of the penis as dangerous to the child, in the second it is considered necessary to its development.

An example of the latter is the following little story, which I have taken from the folklore of the Eskimos. They say that the first child ever born to woman told of his experiences in the womb. In his mother's body he had a narrow but comfortable room, and the way he was fed was, that whenever his parents had intercourse a sweet liquid came out from the penis for his benefit.

THE ŒDIPUS COMPLEX

A boy of five and a half evolved for himself a similar theory; after he had ascertained by questions the function of the umbilical cord in nourishing the child in the womb, he proceeded to identify it with the father's penis, and he took great pleasure in the idea that his father at so early a stage was already caring for him.

Both in the Eskimo legend and the child's corresponding theory it is very interesting to see how the father's rôle as the mother's *lover* is covered and masked by his rôle as *provider*. Probably this implies the repression of a painful thought. That is to say, the discovery—whether instinctive, or from observations, or from early enlightenment—of the true nature of the parents' relations makes the child's feelings about sexuality still more complicated. On the one hand the child too would like to love and have a baby like the adults; on the other, it fears that the consequence of grown-ups' love may be the birth of a fresh rival. Hostile feelings towards a new brother or sister tend to bring about, just as does the rivalry towards the parent of the same sex, repression of sexual wishes and with it the wish for a baby. In trying to repress these wishes a child is helped by the only too frequent remarks of adults about how 'children bring only care and sorrow', 'life is all very well until one has children', and so on. Not seldom, too, children are frightened about the pains of childbirth. Many mothers, anxious to secure due recognition for their deserts, paint the ordeal in vivid colours. Boys then must think themselves villains should they wish to inflict such things on a woman, and girls will suppose that there can be nothing so frightful as to be a mother. The anxiety related to motherhood, and especially to offspring,

THE ŒDIPUS COMPLEX

is in both sexes one of the reasons why in our civilization childbearing has ceased to be a problem-free, natural consequence of instinctual activity.

In conclusion, I revert to what I said in the first chapter about the differing social requirements as to repression among peoples of different levels of civilization. I said that we should see that even among primitive peoples children do not grow up without repression, that indeed they have to renounce their most important instinctual wishes just as our children do. It is in fact so. Those wishes, the fulfilment of which all mankind must deny itself, when taken together form the Œdipus complex. We know of no people among whom it is not forbidden that a girl should unite with her father, a son with his mother. This prohibition is so primeval that certain sociologists like Atkinson and Andrew Lang, preceding Freud, regarded it as a fundamental of the human race as such. Freud demonstrated the prodigious significance of the prohibition in the development of the human psyche; we might say that man is distinguished from the animals by the fact that he has an Œdipus complex, but they have not.

Finally let us recall why Freud named the child's first love the Œdipus complex. In the Greek story King Œdipus killed his father Laios and took his mother Jocasta to wife, by whom he had four children. This legend, which exposes so clearly the wishes existing, according to psycho-analytical evidence, in every human being, is witness at the same time to the fact that these wishes are not a mere invention of modern psychology.

Chapter Three

THE CASTRATION COMPLEX

IN the preceding chapter we considered the condition of the child while dominated by the Œdipus complex. This section—perhaps the most important—of mankind's sexual development lasts roughly from the second to the fifth year. A main characteristic of this stage is the re-grouping of the sexual instincts, so that the genital organs begin to take the leading part in the sphere of sexual satisfaction. Another important manifestation of this period of development is its rich and intense emotional accompaniments. We saw that the child at this age is already capable of passionate love, and also of wild jealousy and hate. We considered the fact that such hostile emotions, felt towards rivals, lead to serious mental conflicts, since they are turned against just those persons whom the child otherwise loves with all its heart. This conflict of feeling is the prime cause for the banishment of the child's first love, and all that is comprised in it—in other words, the Œdipus complex—into the unconscious.

THE CASTRATION COMPLEX

Yet not only paternal prerogatives, but also the child's physical immaturity, ensure that the child's love must remain for ever unsatisfied, and repression is called in against this inner fiasco.

We shall now examine the third main motive for the repression of the Œdipus complex. This third factor is partly intermingled with the others, but its origin is strictly quite separate, and we must go a long way back to find it. First of all, I must recall the observations made in the first chapter, as to the aboriginal, most primitive instinctual disposition of the infant. The first stage of development is characterized by the fact that the various sexual instincts seek satisfaction independently of each other, and this satisfaction is achieved, in great part, without aid from the outside world. At this stage, accordingly, the infant has no need of anybody particular to love, in order to gratify the wishes arising from its primitive sexuality.[1] This comes about the more easily, in

---

[1] [Note by the editor.] This was the generally accepted theory in the early thirties. Since then important developments have taken place, among them that outlined in A. Balint's 'Love for the Mother and Mother-Love' (*International Journal of Psycho-Analysis* 1949, XXX, p. 251; the German original appeared in 1939). For present purposes it is only necessary to note that in that paper the author calls attention to the 'archaic love' between infant and mother, 'the fundamental condition of which is the complete harmony of interests'. This earliest pattern of love is an entirely 'selfish' one, because there is no occasion for 'unselfish' recognition of another self and another self's interests. No knowledge on the infant's part of external reality is required. The pattern may occasionally recur without harm in later life, e.g. during sexual intercourse, but the dangers for both infant and mother of prolonging it as the preponderant form of relationship, beyond the infantile situation, are plain; one of them is the emergence in the child of excessive auto-erotism, referred to in the present text. The author, who recognized the archaic attachment to the mother as the first form of human

THE CASTRATION COMPLEX

that at this age the infant regards the part of its environment which is essential to its needs and is in fact at its disposal—e.g. its mother's breast—as part of its own self.

On this foundation is built in a child that attitude towards itself which we may term self-love, or, more technically, *narcissism*.[1]

Thus, a child's first love-object is itself. Although it later learns to love others too, yet it remains true to this first self-love all its life long. Narcissism may properly be regarded as the sexual component of the instinct of self-preservation. In every disappointment in love, or in any other loss—even in disturbance of physical health—we seek a refuge in this emotion and find consolation in it.[2]

It would take us too far from our path to explore the important problems of narcissism in detail. It comprises a large and significant group of manifestations of which I only wish here to select one part: the aspect of childish narcissism connected with the genitals.

Freud demonstrated that the sexual organs take over a leading rôle, becoming the main conduit for the sexual stimuli arising from various sources by the third or fourth

relationship, would no longer regard auto-erotism as the infant's primary state, and this advance in insight has many important consequences; these however do not vitiate the general observations and conclusions given in the present work.

[1] The term narcissism is derived from the Greek legend, in which it is told that a beautiful young man named Narcissus was so attracted by his reflection, as he leant over the water, that he tried to embrace it, and falling in was drowned; but the gods changed him into the narcissus which grows by the waterside.

[2] In old crude comedies we often find tragi-comic situations where a sudden toothache or colic kills all other emotion in the fiery suitor or fond bride.

THE CASTRATION COMPLEX

year. The great significance of the genitals is particularly manifested in the self-gratification (masturbation) which recurs at that age with renewed vigour.

We have already discussed the significance of masturbation in connection with the Œdipus complex; let us now consider what this method of satisfaction signifies from the standpoint of the childish ego. For one thing, we may say the same thing here as of thumb-sucking, that genital masturbation is a form of satisfaction which makes the child independent of its environment. This is the main foundation for that high regard which a child feels for its own sexual organs. Since Ferenczi's investigations on genital development, this aspect of the matter has been still further illuminated from another side. According to his theory the genitalia acquire the principal rôle by absorbing the excitability of the other erogenous zones. He says 'The erogenous parts of the body confide their functions, in the course of development, to the genitals as a sort of managing director, so that the latter become responsible on behalf of the whole organism for the discharge of sexual tension.' In this way the sexual organ comes to represent the whole pleasure-giving properties of the body. The most important consequence of this centralization of the discharge of sexual tension is, in the mental field, that the child's love for its own self finds primary expression in a high valuation of its own genitals. One might, in fact, say 'the child loves its own sexual organ like itself'.

The following little anecdote of a boy of five illustrates this narcissistic estimation for the genitals. The family were celebrating the promotion of a newly-fledged subaltern, and

THE CASTRATION COMPLEX

the little boy stood in front of him and admired his sword. Then drawing himself up he announced proudly 'I've got a wee-wee too!'

The narcissism associated with the genitals arouses a child's interest in the sexual organs of other people. This finds expression in researches which are on the one hand pleasurable, but on the other lead to bitter disappointments. Comparison with the large penis of animals or adults casts the first shadow over a child's self-confidence. It is true that a boy consoles himself with the thought that his own member will grow big in time, but the very acknowledgment of this consolation is a bitter pill to swallow for a small child who was rejoicing in his own adequacy. Anyone may have noticed how to children at a certain age—usually about three or four—the remark 'Later on, when you're grown-up . . .' is unwelcome. Often they answer in tones of heartfelt conviction 'But I'm grown-up now'. That 'later on' implies the unacceptable fact that the child is 'still little', and so cannot compete with the grown-ups.

The first consequences of this comparison with the great advantages of grown-ups are as a rule envy and anger, which however are allied with respect and admiration. An instructive example of this is the story of a boy of four, who one day saw his father's penis. He exclaimed in surprise 'Goodness, have you got one too?' Some time later he began to play with his hand in his father's trouser pocket. When the latter asked him what he was feeling for, he answered with some confusion, 'I didn't mean to tickle you, I only wanted to rub it away.' Later the parents noticed that the boy took uncommonly long in the lavatory. His father went in to him, and the child greeted him with the words 'Look, I have just the same sort of trousers as you'.

The child's first surprise exclamation may be considered as merely expressive of astonishment. But in wanting to 'rub it away' there is already a sign of hostile feeling, and the remark about the trousers being the same finally shows clearly that the little would-be master is not willing to abandon his competition. I know of a similar instance in the case of a little girl of three, who once when she saw her mother's breasts at first admired their size, and then said 'I'll take them away from you'. She was successfully soothed, however, by the assurance that she too had breasts which in time would grow just as big.

We see from these examples that such comparisons rouse mixed feelings in children, and evoke the struggle in them for maintaining their faith in their own completeness and adequacy. But this faith becomes more and more threatened. A breach in childish self-confidence is already made by the mere realization that there are beings with a larger penis; this is the unavoidable consequence of acquaintance with the facts of external reality. But education, too, does its part in shaking a child's faith still further. As a rule it is unsparing with open and hidden attacks on a child's sexual organs. It is by no means rare to find parents or nurses, when they want to break a child's habit of masturbation, or the bed-wetting often accompanying it, saying that they will cut off the penis or the offending hand; others again prophesy dire consequences of disease, idiocy, stunted growth and so on.

THE CASTRATION COMPLEX

Parents are often surprised at the way in which children, who have been happy, frank and bold up to the age of three or four, then turn quiet, reserved and timid. They have no idea of the cause of the change. Least of all do they suspect that it originates in the emotional shock felt by the child when it is led to believe that masturbation, which heretofore it has regarded as a simple and natural way of obtaining pleasure, may bring in its train ruin, disease, and for a boy even the loss of the penis itself. The child is faced here with an apparently insoluble dilemma. The genital organ is precious to a child on account of just that pleasure which the adults try to take from it with their menaces.

We can only estimate the full import of these open and veiled threats when we realize that it is just at this point that the child is most vulnerable. Just as a vain man regards the most trifling lack of attention towards him as a real insult, the child feels it as a serious slight if it so happens that the existence of his member seems to be disregarded. This high esteem for his genitals is thus at the root of the exaggerated susceptibility to anxiety, under pressure of which a child will take as an attack or a threat even things which are by no means so intended.

An example of this is the following story of a small boy aged about two and a half. To make the point clear I must mention that he was a great thumb-sucker, and—probably because of this—hardly masturbated at all. It became necessary to operate on him for rupture, and he was carefully prepared for the event, but so as not to frighten him too much the word 'cut' was avoided, and all he was told was that 'his tummy would be put right'. But—strikingly

THE CASTRATION COMPLEX

enough—the child nevertheless said himself that he was going to be put right by the barber with his scissors. On the day of the operation this conversation ensued: the child, while he was being dressed, took hold of his penis and asked his mother 'What is this?' 'That's what you do wee-wee with'. 'It's the wee-wee?' 'Yes'. 'Will they put it right too?' 'No, it's quite all right. It doesn't need putting right'. The little boy repeated his last question several times, and on being always reassured in the same way went off quite happily to the nursing-home.

The striking feature in this example is that the child showed no worry about his tummy, but was only frightened for his penis. And it is also noteworthy that this was the first occasion when he felt the necessity of giving this part of his body a separate name. Such christening is however a sure sign of increased love and attachment.

This illustration shows clearly how the instinct of self-preservation is made to serve the purposes of the pleasure-principle. The child instinctively tries to safeguard that part of his body which seems to him most precious as a source of pleasure.

The fact that severe anxiety about the penis can be aroused in boys so easily has yet another root however, which although secondary is nevertheless important; this is the child's *aggressiveness*. The little boy who reacts to the sight of his father's penis with the impulse to take it away from him has good reason to suppose that his father is capable of punishing him for this wish in like fashion. At this point the fear for the penis—the so-called *castration complex*—links up with the Œdipus complex. This form of the castration

THE CASTRATION COMPLEX

complex applies naturally only to boys. We shall consider later what corresponds to it in the case of girls.

The little boy finds that his longing for his mother may lead to an erection. This is the more so, because the more intensive masturbation occurring at this age is especially linked with these phantasies. Masturbation-phantasies are among the most deeply repressed contents of the mind, which as a rule can only be recovered by very thorough-going analysis. In the analysis of these phantasies Freud discovered the *fear of castration* as the most powerful motive for repression of the Œdipus complex.

Two powerful sets of feelings evoke this anxiety, so significant in its later repercussions. One is grounded in the child's self-love, which reaches its peak in his high regard for his penis. Under the influence of the Œdipus situation the penis, which heretofore was only a means for narcissistic discharge of pleasure, acquires also an important significance in respect of love for others. The little boy experiences erection when grown-ups fondle him; he especially likes to show off his member before his mother, and, last but not least, phantasies connected with his mother accompany his masturbation. These feelings we may call the positive group: *undisturbed self-confidence and happy love.*

To the second group belong the *rivalry* arising from comparison and the *wish to take* the larger penis away from others. This covetous wish is in the Œdipus situation directed particularly against the father. The emotions about the penis lead to the result that the child takes the rejection of his love as a belittling also of his penis. For the little lover regards his father's preferential position with his mother as the consequence of his possessing a larger penis. Thus his love engenders in him the same wish as does his narcissistic sensitivity, namely to get the father's penis for himself, so as to win his mother. This, then, is the set of negative emotions: *threatened self-confidence* and *envious hate towards the father*.

In discussing the Œdipus complex we saw that the child wishes for the death of its rival. Now we can add that this wish, in the case of a boy, implies the castration of the father.

Having regard to all this, it becomes readily understandable that any threat directed against a child's physical integrity may have such a frightening effect. Like a criminal who sees the police after him everywhere, the child under the weight of his guilty conscience expects his deserved punishment from every quarter. But this punishment, for the little primitive being who thinks in the fundamental terms of 'an eye for an eye, a tooth for a tooth', can be nothing else but castration. This is the third motive we mentioned—and, we may certainly add, the decisive one—for the repression of the Œdipus wishes. Love and narcissism here stand in opposition. Repression denotes the victory of self-esteem over love. The little boy renounces his mother, so as to preserve his penis intact.

Since I am here discussing emotions and impulses which very rarely reach the level of consciousness, and since in the scope of a book such as this it is impossible to give the convincing evidence available from a full analysis, I will try to illustrate from ethnological examples how general to the human mind, and how far-reaching, are the emotions we have just discussed. For we may deduce from ethnological evidence that the drama which takes place today in our children's unconscious minds was at one time stern reality. In prehistoric times the father was actually slain by his sons when they grew up; the deed was done so that the sons might acquire the women (their fathers' wives, i.e. their mothers) for themselves. A strikingly convincing survival of this primeval struggle is the custom still existing among some peoples of partially mutilating, or in some way marking, boys at the stage of puberty before they are admitted to the circle of grown men. The process is very often, and probably originally was always, performed on the sexual organ. It is carried out, by sons who have become fathers, upon their own boys who are approaching manhood, in order to frighten the latter from the assault planned in the past by these fathers upon their own sires—for which they had been penalized in the same way.

These initiation rites for the youths are thus as it were a counterpart of the battles in the primal horde, from which another direct offshoot is the rite of slaying the king. In this, the holy king or priest has to be slain, when his vigour declines, as a rule by his successor (with some peoples the favoured son or nephew must be both successor and executioner of his father or uncle). In this way it is secured that the important post is obtained by young and vigorous candidates. Analysis of these customs however clearly demonstrates that the power by which the king assures the wellbeing and increase of his people is the power of procreation. According to our theory, in the primal horde one powerful father held all the women in subjugation to himself, and accordingly the perpetuation of the race depended in the literal sense upon his potency. The belief in the miraculous

THE CASTRATION COMPLEX

powers of kings is thus only a reflection of the power of the original procreator. The ritual slaying of the king corresponds psychologically, and also in a certain sense historically, with parricide.

I have been obliged to retail these somewhat gruesome and incredible facts, in order to be able to give an idea of the significance of the active and passive castration phantasies for both individual and social development. And my outline was further necessary to make intelligible the burden of guilt which weighs upon the small boy when he masturbates. We saw that the phantasies which arouse guilt and the fear of retribution are most closely connected with masturbation. Yet just this anxiety often drives a child to still greater indulgence, since he feels compelled to keep on convincing himself in this way of the fact that his member is still intact and capable of erection.

Education is faced here by a conflict which it can hardly mitigate, but which, if unnecessarily intensified, may have a very damaging effect on the child's development. It is most important that parents and teachers should have tact in dealing with the problem of masturbation. For this purpose we must in the first place try to get a clear idea as to what masturbation exactly is. This is a point still clouded by obscurity and for that reason also the subject of widely differing views. Even among the educated classes the belief still goes deep that masturbation is somehow an especially dangerous and damaging thing (as witness, for example, the expression 'self-abuse'). Many seriously believe what they tell their children about the illnesses that may result. But educators should be brought to know that their opposition

THE CASTRATION COMPLEX

to masturbation is motivated not so much by the practice itself as by its *accompanying unconscious phantasies*. These phantasies comprising, besides wishes concerned with the loved person, merciless impulse towards the rival, cause the profound feeling of *guilt* which survives also in the minds of adults, and hinders the latter from forming a right judgment of children's behaviour.

Yet, even if we can set aside the misunderstanding and ignorance brought about by our own repressions, we are still on doubtful ground. The problem of education, referred to in the first chapter, 'how far repression is unavoidably required for the maintenance of our culture', i.e. how much restriction on instinct must be demanded of our children, is nowhere so sharply posed as in the matter of masturbation. It seems almost as though the prohibition of masturbation is a mainstay of our system of upbringing. On the other hand one may readily observe that there is almost no other area of the mind where sanctimoniousness, the division between what may and may not be spoken of, and the contrast between the children's and adults' world, is so pronounced. It seems therefore that masturbation lies at the centre of the worst conflict between instinctual disposition and the adaptation to civilization. Psycho-analysis is indeed far from having found the perfect concordat for this struggle. Yet we can by now formulate a few guiding principles which, it is to be hoped, may help towards a happier issue.

First, it must be emphasized that masturbation is the first and natural manifestation of genital erotism, and therefore quite certainly a phase of sound and normal development. The genital aspect is the side of sexuality which in normal

THE CASTRATION COMPLEX

adults takes first place, and thus masturbation must be allowed its due importance as an essential stepping-stone to normal sexuality. Yet how great this 'due importance' should be is a practical question not easy to answer. We may, however, in general terms assign to it a measure of self-gratification which will not restrict the child's capacity for the current tasks of life (school, play, companionship etc.); this much should be tolerated, for the complete absence of masturbation is as much a sign of disorder as is over-indulgence in the practice. If, that is, as a result of frightening deterrents (which are often coupled with the stimuli which lead to masturbation) genital satisfaction apparently fails to develop in a child, we may be sure, in view of all we know about the nature of instincts, that the obverse of the medal will not be lacking, and that the child, in place of the normal outlet which is denied him, will find other and devious means of satisfying his sexuality.

It may be objected here that *sublimations* are just such deviations, i.e. alternative means of discharge for sexuality. It is quite true that we must all sublimate; such solutions of life's problems as school, games, companionship, work, are in great part carried through by means of sublimated sexual energy. But should sublimation be the sole aim of education? Even assuming the possibility of a complete sublimation of sexual energy before the marrying age (which is the question at issue, since after that everything is again permissible), we must ask ourselves whether happiness, satisfaction, and sexual enjoyment are not just as important things.

Freud remarked often throughout his publications that a high proportion of the neurotics he treated were endowed with considerable intellectual gifts, and possessed a moral sense above the average; and in the sexual sphere they had allowed themselves too little rather than too much freedom. In order to cure them it was necessary to demolish partially the sublimation they had achieved, so as to re-establish, with the sexual energy so liberated, their previously diminished ability to enjoy life. There is now so much experience available on this point that we may safely say that *overdone sublimation of instincts* leads either to illness or to loss of enjoyment of life, often making things intolerable not only for the individual concerned but for the people surrounding him. And sublimations in themselves are not always valuable. How many children, for example, are with pain and grief taught music when they obviously have no talent for it, or in other ways are forced unnecessarily into a pattern which does not fit them. And worse harm than is done by enforced learning is caused by exaggerated and over-strict standards of morals and manners. Beginning with the dress which must not be dirtied, right up to sexuality which must be suppressed and ignored, we establish seemingly impassable barriers, which shut children off from all simple enjoyment of life. The whole world seems to them ruled by a strict governess, who says 'We are not put here to enjoy ourselves'.

Yet, having pleaded for the cause of natural joy in life, we must pause to hear the other side, and consider why those concerned with upbringing are so perturbed over the matter, and so sure that any indulgence in masturbation is dangerous for a child's development. This apprehensiveness is at bottom no more than an acknowledgment of the fact we have already emphasized, that we are concerned here

THE CASTRATION COMPLEX

with a powerful and almost invincible manifestation of instinct. Educators seem convinced that masturbation is something so pleasurable that if it is allowed free play it must lead to immoderate indulgence. On this account it seems to be generally accepted that one cannot go too far in efforts to suppress the practice. Those in charge of children take the attitude of the gipsy who beat his son every day, whether he had done wrong or not, because, as he said, the days when he had done nothing would make up for the days when he had not been found out. In fact, there is almost nothing which is so easy to keep secret as masturbation. Educators are well aware of this, and hope by threats to ensure that a child will police its own activities.

So the practical question which forms a real background to educators' fears may be put thus: how can one combine leniency towards a child with prevention of its falling into excessive indulgence in masturbation? But instead of replying directly, I shall substitute another question, and say 'what are the causes of a child's excessive masturbation?'

To be able to answer this I would recall that masturbation is no simple physical activity, but a *complex psychical performance*, deriving a main contribution from phantasies representing the child's first love. We know, too, that these love phantasies are constantly under the oppression of anxiety and guilt. Masturbation is not only the natural concomitant of the phantasies themselves, but the consolation for the painful feelings which go with them (just in the same way as we have seen in connection with thumb-sucking). Thus the greater the burden of fear and guilt, the more needed is the consolation afforded by masturbation. It follows that

THE CASTRATION COMPLEX

it is by no means certain that freedom to indulge can alone be the original cause of excessive masturbation; menaces and frightening deterrents may easily have the same result.

Another important cause is *petting and spoiling*. Many people maintain that spoiling and freedom are the same, but in reality they are fundamentally different. To spoil a child means, in fact, that one holds out to it the expectation of fulfilment of just such wishes as can never be fulfilled. Strangely enough, anxiety may be aroused by indulgent spoiling as much as by threats and prohibitions. This is partly explicable by the fact that pampering and fondling often go hand in hand with strict forbidding of masturbation, but partly also by the unfulfillable nature of children's wishes. We must not, that is, forget that a child longs for more than it can, with its immature development, achieve. Love-games in bed, playful references by the mother to her 'little husband' or by the father to 'his little wife', all in the last resort constitute for the child a demand beyond its capacity. For the child the thing is far too important to be taken as a pleasantry. Thus spoiling, over-indulgence, both for boys and girls deals in effect a blow to their narcissism, and in the case of boys evokes anxiety about the penis.

While castration-anxiety is related originally to the father, under the effect of the Œdipus complex, indulgent spoiling results in an important change in the content of this anxiety. Where there is no opposition, the boy feels in effect that the main danger comes from his mother instead of his father—for it is she who, by not treating him as a full sexual partner, shakes his confidence in himself. He cannot be a real man, if his mother does not accept him as such. So we see that the father who retreats before the advance of his small rival, and yields—even jokingly—his place with the mother, is doing the child as little service as the parent who sternly cuts down his son's attempts to appear a man.

Thus we may recapitulate our advice about masturbation as follows. It should be permitted up to a certain point, that is, so long as it does not injure a child's capacity for social development. But to keep it within these bounds, we must take care that neither by over-strictness nor over-indulgence is the child driven to find relief through excessive self-gratification. If we observe that a child's masturbation seems over-intensified we should not react with threats or punishment, but first try to find out exactly 'what the child is doing it for'. Of course this cannot always be ascertained or prevented. A departure of the parents, an unwonted sleeping-arrangement, even a new and stimulating kind of game, may motivate intensified masturbation. Since in such cases it is usually only a matter of temporary changes it seems wise to take no particular notice, and only to interfere where a more permanent change in a child's behaviour seems to be involved. And here, too, tact and gentleness are of the first importance. As we have seen in connection with thumb-sucking, we need here also to make every effort to ensure that a child's world is made enjoyable to the child. We should never lose sight of the fact that masturbation is not a deliberate naughtiness, but a help provided by nature against yearning misery, fright, loneliness, or the excitement induced in a child by over-done fondness. So the first thing to do is to remove the causes which make a child need this consolation. Only then can we effectively set about reducing the excessive preoccupation by means of admonitions, distractions, explanations, rewards for self-control, and so on.

Let us return now to the theme of castration-anxiety. As we have seen, a strange process is in operation here, which leads in the end to the result that *both parents* become objects of anxiety for the son. He fears castration from his father on account of his own aggressive desires. But the mother too plays the rôle of one who may castrate him, since she does not acknowledge his full manhood; here the child is frightened by the immoderation of his desires, to which he is not yet equal. This is the root of the *fear of women*, which influences the attitude towards women of the whole male sex. Woman as a creature of riddles, mystery, ruin, and terror is the direct offspring of the castration complex united with the Œdipus complex.

In this connection I must mention yet another feature of femininity which is frightening to a little boy—the female genitals. One of the most general beliefs of childhood is that there is only one kind of sexual organ, the penis. It frequently happens that when a small boy sees a little girl naked he either disbelieves his own eyes or offers consolation with the remark that 'it will soon grow'. The consolation is naturally in the first place for himself, for the fact that there are people who have no penis is so alarming for a little boy that he tries to mitigate it somehow for his own reassurance. An expedient, based similarly on self-deception, for dealing with this discovery is for a boy to suppose that he himself was originally a baby girl, and turned into a boy as he grew bigger. He hopes therefore that little girls are only belated in this process. When he finally becomes convinced that the

THE CASTRATION COMPLEX

difference between the sexes is unalterable, this knowledge greatly contributes to his taking seriously the threats of removal of his penis, etc., which earlier he perhaps thought incredible. The female sexual organ appears to him as a cut, a wound, and the girl a creature who has been punished for masturbation by mutilation.

Little girls react differently in many respects to the difference between the sexes. When a little girl sees a playmate's or brother's penis she concludes without hesitation that he has something which she does not possess, and she envies it. It is often told, either as a joke or a true anecdote, how a small girl on seeing a boy passing water exclaimed wistfully 'How very convenient!'

A mother of a two-year-old girl related the following amusing but instructive incident. After the birth of a baby brother the little girl began an odd game while being bathed. She took the bath-thermometer and first put it between her legs, then held it against her abdomen, and finally threw it crossly away, exclaiming 'It doesn't fit!'

Another mother one day found her little girl, who was aged two and a half and had two elder brothers, crying bitterly in a pool in the bathroom. When asked why she was so upset, the child replied 'Mummy, when shall I be able to do my little job like the boys? I keep trying, but I never manage it'.

And a little girl, also about two years old, was caught by her mother earnestly trying to 'make' a penis for herself with a pencil.

We cannot but be struck by the fact of how comparatively readily and frankly little girls express their feelings about the penis, whereas little boys usually seek refuge in denial of the facts. The explanation is not far to seek. Anxiety, fear, plays a much smaller part with girls than with boys. The girl, in fact, has nothing to lose; her fright, so to speak, is already behind her. Rather, she is envious and hurt because she has not been properly completed. For since children at this early age have no clear notion of the limits on the power of grown-ups, they believe with conviction that the latter could help the situation if they only wanted to. Little girls in fact suppose, just as do little boys, that everybody must have a penis, and they believe their mother has one too and has only behaved like a cruel stepmother in not letting her little daughter have one.

This hostile feeling of grievance against the environment which in the first instance is expressed in hate and reproaches towards the mother, finally brings out a feeling of anxiety and guilt in girls, too, as do hate and envy of the father in boys. But there remains the difference, that the boy is threatened by the risk of losing something that he does possess, whereas the girl is requiring something she has never had. Thus the girl's anxiety is purely fear of retaliation on account of her own aggressive desires, while in the boy there is additionally a proneness to anxiety in reference to the most precious part of his body. The envy felt by girls incidentally contributes to the intensity of the fear of the female sex felt by boys, which has been mentioned above. It is also at the root of the spiteful and predatory attitude towards men in general which is apt to be displayed on occasion even by the most loving women.

The dissatisfaction of the small girl with her own sexual

organ has an interesting repercussion on her narcissism. We have spoken of the fact that genital masturbation is the source of narcissistic high esteem for the sexual organ. How does this esteem fare in conjunction with dissatisfaction over that very organ? We may conjecture that feminine masturbation is perhaps never so highly pleasurable as in the male case, and that for this reason the predominance of the genital zone is not so pronounced in the female sex as in the male. The phenomenon of *feminine vanity* supports this hypothesis. The difference between feminine and masculine vanity is that in the boy, in spite of the threats hanging over him, the genitals are the main vehicle for his narcissism, while in the little girl this rôle is undertaken by her whole body. Boys yearn for long trousers, a collar and tie, etc., so that they may be looked on as men; little girls are little coquettes and mean to be, as they are, 'attractive'. The characteristic feminine vanity shows itself as a rule very early on, and is probably a defence against the feeling of defectiveness.

Having regard to all this, we may better understand why such an apparently disproportionate emotion is aroused in little girls if a mother too strictly and too early opposes their manifestations of feminine vanity. It matters just as much to a little girl that she should be attractive, as to the little boy that he should be regarded as a man. It is not easy, indeed, to find the golden mean here. Just as the boy must keep in mind that as yet he is little and has still to grow up and learn, before he can be a man—and yet must not feel that the struggle for manhood is hopeless; so does every little girl need to be able to believe that she is attractive, although at the same time we have to let her recognize the

THE CASTRATION COMPLEX

deficiencies which must be made up before she can succeed in the full rôle of a woman. This self-confidence can never be harmful to a little girl, and indeed it is justified, since every woman is attractive to the man who loves her. To even the plainest woman can come the knowledge that she is attractive, if education in self-depreciation has not deprived her of her natural armoury.

A mother noted in her diary that her three-year-old daughter went into tantrums of rage if she ever looked into the mirror at the same time as her child. And she never wanted to get dressed when her mother was there, but would sooner struggle, for however long, alone with her buttons and fastenings. This odd behaviour dated from an occasion when her mother had countered some praise from a passing stranger by saying 'Don't take any notice of what the lady says, you're not very pretty really'. The child reacted quickly against her mother's deprecatory remark, and as the upshot showed, 'turned against her' in a very unexpected way.

It is not easy to see why such moderate, even trivial, 'educative' measures should be able to evoke such strong hostile reactions. And yet such instances are by no means rare, especially in the relationship between mother and daughter. We have observed already that little girls feel rivalry towards their mother, because of their love for their father, and that they look on her in this respect as an enemy; added to this is the reproach to the mother for not having given them a penis. If, then, the mother acts in such a way as to deprive the little girl of her great consolation, that without being a boy she is still attractive, the child's anger begins to look fully justified.

THE CASTRATION COMPLEX

Yet the little girl's grievance against her mother for not having created her as complete as a boy is still rather puzzling. Why do little girls direct their complaints precisely against the mother, and why are they so difficult to pacify even when they learn that their mother herself has no penis? One little girl, for example, who already knew where babies come from, said to her mother 'If you had only kept me a bit longer in your tummy, I'd have grown one'. Envy and narcissistic grievance seem an insufficient explanation. We may suspect that the person of the mother herself has a special significance here. It is the *love for her mother* that causes the gravest difficulty for the little girl. For the daughter, just as for the son, the mother is the first and most important object of love. The very first love both for boys and girls originates at the mother's breast. But while the boy can at least imagine in phantasy that one day, when he is grown, he can marry his mother, and take his father's place with her, the girl must early become aware that she can never mean as much as a man to her mother. And soon comes the knowledge that men in general receive greater regard, and that most parents want especially to have a son. Remarks such as 'it's *only* a girl' have made many childish hearts heavy.

All these disappointments tend directly towards making the little girl give up her first love, exchanging it for love of the father. Yet this is a case of 'easier said than done'; the path to the goal of womanliness is indeed a thorny one, leading through narcissistic sufferings and disappointments in love. Nevertheless, the girl-pilgrim's progress to this point is accomplished quite early. She renounces the wish to be

THE CASTRATION COMPLEX

husband to her mother, and wants instead to have a husband for herself, as her mother has. A pretty example of this is a remark reported by the mother of a five-year-old daughter, who had taken to neglecting her little girl-friend in favour of a small boy. When questioned by her mother about this, she asked in turn, 'Well, Mummy, who do you have most fun with, Grannie or Daddy?'

It is interesting about this answer that although the little girl was asked about her friend, she answered as though she had to defend herself against a charge of disloyalty towards her mother. The mother had in fact left her own mother in order to live with 'Daddy', and so the little girl, too, could love a boy instead of her female friend (the equivalent of the mother). Behind it lies the reproach 'you have preferred men (Daddy) to women (me), so I too may prefer men'.

The wish to be a boy stems therefore not only from hurt narcissism, but perhaps even more from the *wounded love of the little girl for the mother*, whom she wants for herself just as much as a boy does. Thus it happens that, even before the mother is seen as a rival to the daughter, a feeling of enmity arises in the little girl, which is nothing else than the anger of a finally rejected lover. We may summarize this by saying that girls, like boys, feel 'man-like' in their love for their mother, and they envy boys because they have more prospect of attracting their mother.

Let us now try to trace the obscure development of little girls a little further. The little girl in her anger turns from her mother, and for a time hopes that her father will fulfil her wishes and needs. Since children at an early age know or suspect that a mother gets babies from the father, the original

THE CASTRATION COMPLEX

wish changes into a longing which comes nearer to reality, namely that *the father will also present the little girl with babies.* We must not be deluded, in dwelling on the agreeable aspect of this situation, into forgetting that the little girl's wish for babies has as yet little to do with love. She wants babies in the first place as a compensation for the missing penis.[1]

This is why small girls are in such a hurry in the matter. I once overheard a conversation between two five year olds on the point. The boy, who had recently learned how babies come, tried to console his girl playmate who wanted above all to be a boy. 'Don't cry over not being a boy', he said, 'later on you'll be a Mummy'. But the little girl was not satisfied with this glimpse of a brighter future, and answered sadly 'But at present I've got nothing at all in my tummy, only earth'. (The little girl understood that in order to get a baby the mother received a seed in the way it is planted in the earth.) The boy was a boy already, while she had to wait so long before she could be a mother. At another time she expressed her feeling quite clearly, saying 'While I'm little I want to be a boy, and when I'm big I'll be a Mummy'.

It is asking far too much of a small child to be content with a promise for the distant future, and so it comes about that as a result of the non-fulfilment of the wish for a baby the little girl goes back to her original wish, that is, she again wants to be a boy. So we see that while the boy is always animated by the same wish, to be a man, the girl is

[1] This original, primitive attitude towards the child is probably the foundation for the widespread custom which decrees that a woman may only take her full place and authority when she has borne a son. Through sons, who are indeed a part of themselves, women may take rank with men.

THE CASTRATION COMPLEX

swayed this way and that between the masculine and feminine ideals, and truly has a hard time in being put on the right track by a succession of painful lessons.

In the course of all these struggles and longings the girl, too, finds consolation in masturbation. Just on this account everything that has been said about the educational approach to masturbation applies to both sexes, in spite of the probably differing significance of the sex organ in boys and girls. With girls, as with boys, we must watch lest they are driven to excessive masturbation by wounding of their self-esteem or by too much fondling. In them, too, masturbation is bound up with love-phantasies (the Œdipus complex) and narcissistic phantasies of greatness (arising from the complex of penis-envy). Girls who suffer acutely from the fact of not being a boy create the feeling of having a penis by masturbation of the clitoris. Childish phantasies of pregnancy are just as frequent.[1]

Those who have the upbringing of children have to try, by loving and tactful treatment, to reduce the disappointments suffered by a little girl to their true proportions. She must feel happy enough with her lot as a little girl to be able to bear the fact that she can never be a boy, and has to wait for a long time yet before she can become a mother. It is a bad and frequent mistake, however, to try to lessen

[1] After a psycho-analytical lecture in Berlin, before the Society for Sexual Reform, the lecturer had questions from a number of women as to whether masturbation could cause pregnancy. This remarkable fear has its roots in the masturbation-phantasies of little girls, wherein they wish to be their father's wife and have babies by him. The counterpart is found in the questions of men as to whether masturbation can cause impotence.

THE CASTRATION COMPLEX

the child's sense of impatience by making out that 'childhood is the happiest time of one's life', as a counter to the advantages of being grown-up. Many mothers react to their daughters' tempestuous wish to be women and mothers with laments about the burdens and sorrows of motherhood, about the domination of men, and even about the father's brutality and the pains of child-bearing—without, of course, mentioning the joys for which these trials are the price. This generally has for the girl's development the undesired result that the primitive wish, to become a man, is revived. Many women of the type that imitates men and hates sex have this kind of thing in their history. The mother's plaints have frightened the little girl off from the sexual goal of womanhood, and she must at the same time hate men, who do women so much harm; she means therefore to be as strong or as learned as a man, so that she may take revenge. This solution can naturally never be a successful one, since the most masculine woman will still never be a man. Such women are themselves a standing affront to their own self-esteem, although it is precisely their narcissism which dictates the pattern of their lives.

Still, the greatest difficulties for a girl lie in the *relationship with the mother*. She loves her mother as every child does, and yet mother and daughter persistently find themselves in the position of enemies. The solution of this conflict is a hard task for both daughter and mother. The disunity in the child's heart may try the mother severely in very many ways, since, alongside an extreme and often burdensome dependence, it may be expressed in open hostility. Little girls frequently, for example, make scornful and derogatory remarks about their mother's appearance. While the mother is the most beautiful being in the world for her son, the little girl, both as rival and as rejected lover, seeks to give vent to her offended feelings in criticism. Mothers often do not recognize the disappointed longing that lies behind the apparently unloving behaviour of a daughter, and estrangement is often the consequence. The mother's ambivalence, too, is apt to manifest itself partly by an exaggerated (because guilty) tenderness, and partly in open hostility. In either case the danger arises that the daughter, instead of finding the path away from the mother towards men, remains tied to the mother. Coldness on the mother's part may, because of the child's unappeased love for her, prevent the requisite loosening of the bond between them. The child will still eternally seek, even when grown up, for a mother-substitute, and bring a childish, immature love to the relationship. Yet on the other hand excessive tenderness—since it allows for no discharge of hostile feelings—keeps the child in a perpetual emotional slavery to the mother, hemmed in by potential guilt.

The amicable loosening of the bond between daughter and mother is one of the most difficult tasks of education. For only when the framework of primary, masculine love of a daughter for her mother is successfully demolished can her envious hate towards men be dissipated, and only then is it possible for the little girl to grow up into a woman in the fullest sense of that word.

To sum up, we may say that both castration-anxiety and penis-envy tend to *make love more difficult* for the child, indeed perhaps even to make it turn from love altogether. In both

THE CASTRATION COMPLEX

sexes love seems a menace to self-esteem. For both, love signifies the abandonment of the belief in one's own completeness, adequacy, integrity. The boy has to acknowledge that he is still little, and as yet no match for his father; and the girl must come to terms with the fact that she can never be a man to attract her mother, and yet is also too small to be a wife to her father. So then, with the help of repression of the Œdipus-wishes, which cannot in any event be fulfilled, self-esteem is preserved at the expense of love.

One of mankind's most difficult tasks is to recover, after this major retreat into narcissism which ends the Œdipus-love, the *courage and ability to love again*.

Chapter Four

IDENTIFICATION

1. THE CONQUEST OF THE EXTERNAL WORLD

So far we have been mainly concerned with the *content* of the conflicts of childhood and we have said very little of the ways in which those conflicts are dealt with. And, now that we are approaching that side of the problem, we must for the time being leave the firm ground of direct observation and turn to a more theoretical consideration of the means adopted by children for the solution of their conflicts. I have already referred in passing to a few of these methods: repression, for instance, and displacement, and (something that is akin to the latter) sublimation. Repression enables us to blot out of our consciousness any wishes that have proved incapable of fulfilment, while displacement and sublimation enable some of our instincts to pursue their existence in a new and legitimate sphere. In the course of my remarks upon displacement I hinted at the existence of another method—namely, identificatory thought. I mentioned that displacement is closely related to this peculiarity of primitive thought, to the fact, that is, that children from

IDENTIFICATION

the very first get to know the external world by means of 'identifications'. For instance, a small child will regard any thick mass of material as fæces, and any liquid as urine, because fæces and urine are things that are already familiar to it. One advantage of these identifications is that they enable the child to find substitutes for primitive sources of pleasure that have to be given up under the pressure of education. Thus identificatory thinking is employed for the purpose of avoiding what is unpleasurable and obtaining what is pleasurable, and it aims at transforming a strange and consequently frightening external world into one that is familiar and enjoyable. This is the only way (apart from direct gratification) in which we can approach the external world. And since the relation between the ego and the external world is after all the main problem of all educative measures, it is worth while examining the phenomenon of identificatory thought in all its details.

The ego, and more particularly the primitive 'pleasure ego', plays the principal part in identificatory thinking to a much greater degree than it does subsequently, after the development of what is called 'objective' thinking. For the basis for the earliest identifications is not resemblance to the object (though naturally this plays its part) but the manner in which the object in question enters into relation with the child's instincts. Indeed, this is self-evident: since whatever does not belong to our ego is alien to us, and thus the starting-point for identification must necessarily be our own body or our own instincts.[1]

---

[1] After we have taken mental possession of a portion of the external world by means of identification, mental material which has thus been

IDENTIFICATION

Thus, for instance, a piece of brown paper will remind a four-year-old boy not of a parcel or of anything connected with paper, but of fæces—which is bound to strike an adult as an exceedingly forced comparison. In the same way a running tap usually reminds children of micturating. I have already in an earlier chapter given the instance of a four-year-old boy who identified a soldier's sabre with a penis. So, too, the very widespread infantile theory of birth through the anus is essentially an identification of the process of birth with the familiar process of defæcation. (This explains how it is that this theory so often makes its appearance even when children have been given precise information upon the facts.)

It is obvious that an external world that has been discovered and conquered in such a fashion will be to the last degree egocentric. And this remarkable picture of the world, with the pleasure-ego as its centre, persists in our unconscious all through our lives and constitutes the basis of the anthropomorphism which always lurks in the background even of the most objective and scientific thought.

It is by means of identification that a child makes the acquaintance even of its own body. Here the basis for the identification is afforded by those organs or parts of the body which are at the moment playing the largest part in the attainment of pleasure, either because some particular stage

assimilated can itself serve as a basis for further identifications. So there would seem to be no essential distinction between ego-identification (i.e. identification of the ego with an object) and object-identification (i.e. identification of one object with another). For it is only objects which have already been identified with ourselves that can become the starting-point for further identifications.

of development has been reached or because some external influences have been at work.

A four-year-old girl, for instance, had formerly derived her greatest pleasure from sucking her fingers. She then experimented with genital masturbation, and had recently practised it more frequently. She explained it with the words: 'I'm feeding my bottom.' This strange explanation shows that, even in the case of a pleasurable, and therefore self-explanatory, activity like masturbation, the process requires to be made more familiar by means of identification. (It seems likely that behind the equation of masturbation with feeding, or eating, there lay an earlier comparison between sexual tension and hunger.) It is of course possible that the sense of guilt involved in masturbation also played a part in the child's explanation. If so, she would have been using the identification to pacify not so much herself as her enquiring elders, as though she were saying: 'There's nothing in it really, it's only the same sort of thing as eating'. A very similar, though simpler, example is provided by the little boy who, as was appropriate to his age, was, like her, devoted to sucking his fingers, and called his penis a 'little finger'. On the other hand, a girl used to call the genitals of a boy she played with a 'little nose', and was thus comparing it with an organ that she herself also possessed. In this case the girl was using identificatory thinking to try to soothe the unpleasurable feelings caused by her lack of a penis.

From all of this it seems as though identificatory thinking were in its nature allied to narcissism. But, whereas narcissism never extends beyond the subject's own ego, identifi-

IDENTIFICATION

cation constitutes the bridge that leads across from naked self-love to getting to love reality.

Nevertheless, identification is not yet object-love. The attachment that we form with the external world by means of identification is far better described as a kind of incorporation or assimilation or, inversely, as an extension of the ego. This can be demonstrated very clearly from a child's relation to its toys. It is a remarkable fact, for instance, that the essence of a small child's play consists in the child itself becoming a dog or a motor-car or a railway-train though the corresponding toys are close at hand. Until this mental incorporation has been achieved, the toy remains something alien and frightening. The preference felt by children for a piece of paper or wood, for an empty box or a bit of string, is easily explained by the fact that these things can assume a greater diversity of shape and consequently afford wider possibilities for identification.

A boy I know was positively terrified of toys that have to be wound up and that then move automatically. He only enjoyed playing with them if he himself moved his whole body in unison with the toy. Most instructive in this connection was the way in which a child of about two and a half came to be on friendly terms with a new toy. He was presented with a red india-rubber elephant, but received it with violent dislike and pushed it away with screams and tears. The function of an elephant's trunk was then demonstrated to him by the use of his own arm; he was shown how the end of the trunk worked like his own fingers; and was told how the elephant could squirt water with its trunk, put food into its mouth, and so on. Not until he himself had

IDENTIFICATION

imitated these various movements for some time could he at last be prevailed upon to look at the toy and take it in his hands. It is worth trying to find the meaning of the various details of this everyday episode. The boy's throwing away of the toy and refusal to look at it may without any exaggeration be regarded as the destruction of a strange and troublesome object. Next followed the game with his own arm and fingers, which opened the way to an identification. After this process of mental 'digestion' had been successfully achieved, the object that had been so repellent only a short time before could now be held in the child's hands and felt as something friendly and familiar.

Processes of an exactly similar kind are taking place in an adult when he says that he must 'digest' a new idea before he can 'get on to friendly terms' with it; and to 'explain' something means in fact to facilitate this process of digestion. The game which the child was shown with his arm was an explanation of the elephant's body given in a form appropriate to a child's understanding. But the 'appropriate' form of this explanation lay, as we have seen, in the fact that it made possible an identification with the child's ego. Thus, on the one hand, children's play can be regarded partly as a summation of primitive explanations; and, on the other hand, the intellectual working over of a problem would seem probably always to be a process of identification. This would constitute the inevitable libidinal foundation of knowledge or understanding in general. If this close connection between knowledge and identification in fact holds, it implies that knowing is always *re*-knowing, that is, that we are able to know the external world only as something akin to the ego.

IDENTIFICATION

Thus, as we have seen, in the last resort a child wishes to meet only its own beloved self.

A story of a three-year-old boy will serve to exemplify this. He was afraid of thunderstorms; and one morning after a thundery night it was found that he had wetted his bed. Since he had been trained for some time, this event required a special explanation. The child told his mother what had happened in these words: 'I didn't want to do it. But the sun said I *was* to do it in the bed. I said I wouldn't. But the sun said it does it too'. 'How's that?' asked his mother. 'When it rains, of course'. Here the little boy was trying to get on to friendly terms with the frightening rainstorm by identifying the rain with micturition, which at the same time allowed him to indulge in a pleasure which had long been forbidden.

A child can only get on to friendly terms with toys, with animals, with natural phenomena, as well as with the grown-up people living with him, if he can succeed in identifying himself with them. Identification can accordingly be regarded as a flight from the external world—this flight being carried out by means of our making a larger and larger portion of the external world into a portion of our ego. The further a child advances along this path, with the more things must he become acquainted which were at first disagreeable. This is an instructive instance of the way in which the pleasure principle itself leads to adaptation to reality. A child's one aim is to feel contented. But he is hindered in this by the external world which, by means of constant stimuli, is constantly confronting him with new problems. His way out is identification, by the help of which

IDENTIFICATION

he takes the external world into himself, or, as we may say, assimilates it.

All this leads us to what will undoubtedly seem a paradoxical conclusion, namely, that a child is driven to have recourse to identification above all when he is overcome by painful impressions from which he has no other means of escape. And since running away or getting rid of a disturbing phenomenon is the least practicable method of defence in earliest childhood, identification is incomparably more important at that period of development than at any other time of life. If, therefore, we wish to be quite accurate, we must say, not that a child gets on to friendly terms with something because it reminds him of something else of which he is already fond or which he already knows, but that a child can only become fond of something unknown if he can succeed, by the help of one of his instincts, in identifying it with something known. The common basis of loving and of understanding is identification, and without it both would be impossible.

Loving is not, of course, merely synonymous with identification; on the one hand it is the result of direct instinctual satisfaction, while on the other hand it presupposes a certain degree of sense of reality, which makes it possible to distinguish the ego from the external world. But what does that mean? We must above all not forget that the separation of ego from non-ego is originally effected by the help of painful experiences. We are taught, for instance, that our mother's breast is not a part of our own body by the painful experience that it is not always there when we need it. Loving is thus preceded by anger or, more precisely, by the discovery that

IDENTIFICATION

what gives us satisfaction is an alien and hostile object belonging to the external world. This means that when a child is hungry he is not fond of his mother's breast but angry with it. In order to love it, the child must be able to remember the pleasure which the breast was the means of giving him. Thus loving is essentially gratitude, that is, the maintenance of affectionate feelings even at a time at which direct gratification has ceased.

A good example of a contrary state of things is afforded by the following anecdote, of which the hero is a boy of about six. He was out somewhere on a visit and had been playing very happily with a small dog, so that finally he could not bear the idea of parting with it. When he saw that all was in vain and that he *must* go home without it, he suddenly said: 'Horrid dog! I don't love you!' Here we can see plainly that the child was angry with the bad dog that was the cause of his sorrow at parting.

It commonly happens that on such occasions a child will console himself with the help of identification. He will, for instance, turn himself into a dog and to such good effect that he no longer has the smallest need of the real animal. Thus identification can not only promote the development of loving but can just as easily hinder it: for if we are scared at the suffering which is involved in loving we can turn back to identification, as though to a more primitive form of relationship. But in setting up this secondary identification we have to fight not only against the alien nature of the object but also against an especially evil characteristic that it possesses, namely, the fact that it is not invariably or unconditionally at our disposal. In this case the aim of

IDENTIFICATION

identification is no longer getting to know something that is unknown but replacing something that is missing. I no longer need the bad dog which I had to part with, if I can myself become a dog and so get satisfaction from myself.

The capital distinction between loving and identification lies in the fact that identification is the transforming of a painful, disturbing state of affairs into a pleasurable one, whereas loving is linked to gratification (that is, to something pleasurable) and in such a way that from the gratification we can find strength to tolerate the suffering that is bound up with it. The greater the direct gratification, the less need there is for identification. The other great distinction between identification and loving is that identification tends to do away with the separation between the ego and the external world, while it is a necessary condition of loving that we should recognize the fact that something else exists outside ourselves.

The first important gratification which we obtain through the agency of another person is sucking. Sucking comprises three different kinds of relation: first, an actual incorporation of a portion of the external world; secondly, narcissistic pleasure (since the process occurs at an age at which the separation of ego from non-ego has not yet been completely effected); and, finally, it contains the germ of the first love-relation. During sucking complete peace still reigns between the ego and the external world, between narcissism and object-love. It is the prototype of complete happiness. When we reflect, therefore, that it is precisely in the sphere of oral erotism that a child experiences not only its first great happiness but also its first great shocks (such, for instance,

IDENTIFICATION

as weaning, teething and—last but not least—hunger), we shall more readily understand the great importance of the part played in mental life by identification, which is so closely related to the impulse of oral incorporation. It is common knowledge that small children seek to allay every pain, whether mental or physical, in one and the same way: by taking something into their mouth. The prototype of this mechanism of consolation is the assuaging of hunger—that is to say, sucking. If milk is not in a child's mouth when he becomes hungry, he has a high degree of unpleasurable feeling; and this painful event leads to a sharp differentiation between his ego and the external world. If milk then enters his mouth, this disharmony ceases and the integrity of his ego is re-established. This process, which is in part physiological, is a complete counterpart to the purely mental process which we term identification. Thus identification serves the pleasure principle in two sorts of way: on the one hand, it removes the tension between the ego and the external world, and, on the other hand, its mechanism brings a recollection of the happiness which we enjoyed as sucklings.

Our relation with our own self develops in a manner precisely similar to what we have already described in the case of the ego and the external world. Let us take as our starting-point those cases in which a child feels as something alien to him a part of his body which is causing him pain. We see children holding an injured finger far away from them, being angry with it and not wanting to look at it. Or they talk about the organ that is tormenting them in the third person—'that naughty tummy'—and wish someone would buy them another one, and so on. It is as though this

IDENTIFICATION

behaviour meant: 'I'm fond of myself; but what hurts me is naughty and I don't like it; that's not me at all'. On the one hand, therefore, everything that is not part of the ego is, to begin with, bad and alien, while, on the other hand, there is an inclination to project into the external world everything in the ego that is disturbing. Here, too, in other words, the separation of the ego from the external world proceeds according to the rule: what is good is ego, what is bad is non-ego.

Children will endeavour to get rid of disturbing emotions in the same way by means of projection. For instance, a child of four said to his playmate: 'If you don't leave my toy alone, a man'll come out and be angry'. The child was asked why he did not simply say that he himself would be angry. His answer was: 'Because I don't want to be angry any more'.

Since in the case of physical pains being angry or repudiating the aching part does not, of course, lead to the desired end, the child is once more obliged to take refuge in identification. The result of this process of identification is that he nurses and caresses the aching part. But to this we shall return later.

A similar situation also occurs in the case of psychological injuries. We have already mentioned in connection with the castration complex how easily small children feel insulted, precisely because of their narcissism. After narcissistic injuries of this kind it may happen that a child will so to speak abandon his own self, since he no longer feels any pleasure in his ego. A very common sign of this is that the child assumes a new name and declares that his old ego is dead

IDENTIFICATION

and exists no longer. If after this we call him by his old name the result is usually a bitter outburst of crying or a fit of rage; so that I have found as a rule that people give way to 'strange whims' of this kind on the part of a child. We often find, for instance, that little girls, as soon as they have noticed that they lack something that little boys possess, want to stop being girls. The effect of this is intensified by remarks which they often hear preferring boys to girls. A snub or a sign of dislike may entirely take away a little girl's pleasure in herself. And the same thing may happen to a little boy if he is too bluntly reminded of his weakness and smallness compared with grown-up people. The impenetrable armour which we also call narcissism and which affords the individual his most effective protection against the opinion of others is already something secondary and is already in its essentials the product of a process of identification. When a child finds that he cannot get free from his own imperfect ego, he identifies himself with the people who are fond of him in spite of his imperfections. This origin of secondary self-love gives us a satisfactory explanation of the invulnerability of those who are protected by its armour.

The child's original attitude to the external world may be formulated in these words: 'if you are fond of me, then make me as perfect as I myself feel I am'. At first, for instance, a little girl will be angry because people are fond of her as a little girl and endeavour to use that as a means of inducing her to submit to her lot. Strange as it may seem, she feels this love as hostility. (We frequently come across this same conflict in the pages of modern love stories, where

IDENTIFICATION

the mainspring of the plot consists in a woman feeling her self-respect injured because she is loved 'merely as a woman' and 'not as a human being'.)

Something precisely similar is to be observed in physical suffering. A man who is ill abandons himself in just the same way as a child whose self-respect has been injured. It is as though he were surrendering his now worthless ego to his environment: 'I don't need it any more; please do whatever you like with it'. For the sick adult is, like the child, angry with his environment, as though he were making it responsible for his suffering. Just as a child is angry because she has been brought into the world so small, or because she has been made a girl and not a boy, so does the sick man (or child) nourish a hostile feeling against his environment because it has made him fall ill. This anger is a direct derivative of the mechanism of projection of which I have already spoken in connection with physical pain. We are unwilling to regard as part of our ego anything that is painful or imperfect—anything of which we must feel ashamed; and we therefore do our best to locate either the evil itself, or at least its causes, outside ourself.

The following anecdote offers an amusing example of this. A small boy of five fell down off a piece of furniture. He burst into sobs and tears and complained that his grandfather, who happened to be in another corner of the room, had pushed him over. Instead of admitting his own clumsiness, he looked for a scapegoat with whom he could be heartily angry, whereas, if he had had an understanding of the situation, he would have had to be angry with himself.

Anger with the environment is, as we can see, a protection

IDENTIFICATION

against abandoning the self, or, more correctly, against the narcissistic injury which would be the consequence of understanding. This anger with the environment, on the one hand, and the inclination to self-abandonment, on the other, are the justification for special spoiling in case of illness or other mischance. For it is only by the help of identification with his environment that a person can contrive to love himself even though he is small or ill or humiliated.

Of course we must not forget that the impulse to self-abandonment is counteracted most strongly by—what is the actual basis of primary narcissism—the gratification which a person obtains from his own body: from masturbation in the widest sense of the word. From this point of view masturbation must be regarded as a positively life-saving agency. We shall also understand why it is that masturbation increases at the period at which children have to go through a series of disappointments and humiliations in connection with the Œdipus and castration complexes. Masturbation prevents complete self-abandonment; it assures us, even in times of need, of our love for ourself, which, like all other love, is built up upon gratification.

Thus we see that, in the process of establishing the relation between an individual and the external world, the decisive part is played by identification and love. Loving stands furthest away from the original aim. It demands the greatest possible adaptation to the external world and at the same time makes the greatest breach in primary narcissism. Identification is the most primitive method of recognizing external reality; it is, in fact, nothing less than mental mimicry. Its necessary preconditions are an unbroken

IDENTIFICATION

narcissism, which cannot bear that anything should exist outside itself, and the weakness of the individual, which makes him unable either to annihilate his environment or to take flight from it.

2. THE CHILD AND HIS EDUCATORS

From a practical point of view there is one exceedingly important special case of the relation between an individual and the external world, namely the relation between a child and his educators. For small children their parents and educators represent an immense power, the loss of whose love and goodwill is almost the same thing as the gravest mortal danger. It is easy to see why this is so, for it is a self-evident implication of children's complete physical and mental dependence. If a child were not helpless, he might, for instance, if his parents refused to give him something he wanted, say to himself: 'I'm going away: I don't like it here'. Since this solution is impossible for him, anger becomes a forbidden luxury, and he is obliged instead to resort to the same method in relation to his prohibiting and hence disagreeable parents as he has previously been able to use against the hostile and mighty external world—namely, to the method of identification. On the other hand, however, we know that these same parents are also a source of intense gratification for him and for that very reason are his first and most important love objects. Thus it is that parents come to bear the weight of the most vital, because the strongest and most permanent, attachments. We love them

IDENTIFICATION

because they bring us pleasure and we identify ourselves with them as being the powerful representatives of the frustrating external world. Accordingly, in relation to parents, love and identification are so much intermingled that any clear differentiation between the two seems hopeless. And the position is made still more difficult by the fact that these two types of relation, which are so fundamentally different in their essence, make use for the most part of the same forms of expression. Love towards parents is not only something that is felt spontaneously but also something that is strictly forbidden. An educator is as a rule very little concerned as to the manner in which a child is attached to him; it is enough for him to know that such an attachment exists and is utilizable for the purposes of education. And yet, as we shall see presently, even from the practical point of view the distinction between the two forms of relation is not a matter of indifference. But I will first endeavour to draw a rough outline picture of the way in which love and identification are intermixed, and of how they alternate in the course of a child's development.

According to the schematic formula of the Œdipus complex, a small boy should love his mother and identify himself with his father. And this is in general the case. The boy's mother is after all the source of gratification and his father is the powerful rival against whom he cannot defend himself successfully either by attack or by flight, so that he is eventually obliged to resort to identification. The most familiar form taken by this identification is where the boy tries to do whatever his father is doing, imitates his father's movements and little habits, etc. It is true, of course, that the repressed

IDENTIFICATION

Œdipus wish also re-emerges in this identification: the little boy is becoming his father—that is, he is becoming his mother's husband. The hostile intention which was the precursor of the identification finds its expression in such remarks as: 'if I was Daddy, Daddy'd be a baby and I'd push him in the pram'. What I have said applies also, *mutatis mutandis*, to little girls. A girl is happy if she can imitate her mother in respect of her clothes or in the way she wears her hair; and it appears too that she would like to have a husband just like Mummy's. I once heard a young woman doctor say of her parents: 'Getting married wasn't much of a job for Mummy, she got married to Daddy'.

Differences in family circumstances, in the character of the parents, in their educational methods and in the possibilities of gratification open to a child can of course lead to the most various consequences. But, besides these, there are other factors of a much more general nature that can alter the picture to a greater or less extent. For instance, the mother or nurse is the chief source of pleasure for children of *both* sexes in their earliest years. Yet during the processes of weaning and of training in cleanliness the same person becomes a most disagreeable creature from the child's standpoint. At that period the child withdraws his love from her and directs it instead to his father, who as a rule has no share in this early education. One often hears a mother complaining of her baby's ingratitude because he prefers his father, although he only spares an occasional leisure moment to him, whereas he has not the least regard for his mother, who devotes the whole day to him. For older children, on the contrary, their father as a rule once again becomes the representative of harsh reality, while their mother is affectionate and indulgent. Alterations of this kind in the part played by parents bring about now an intensification, now a diminution in the effect of the Œdipus and castration complexes. These two complexes, moreover, do not operate entirely in the same sense. As we have seen, for instance, a little boy will usually associate his father with prohibition but his mother with failure. This applies equally to little girls. Her mother appears as a prohibiting force, but, since she has been disappointed by her father, she has no alternative but to turn away, to a greater or lesser extent, from *both* her parents. And in fact we find that after the climax of the Œdipus complex there follows a calming-down of the feelings that have been raging around the parents. Under the pressure of its various disappointments the child withdraws its love in part from its parents and turns to the external world—in a wider sense of the word. Then follows the period in which friendships begin, the desire for knowledge increases and the personality develops.

The child's 'psychological emigration' from his parents' house is occasionally expressed in attempts at an actual emigration. I myself once witnessed something of the sort in the case of a boy of three. The child lived near me and I only knew him by sight. One night his mother gave birth to a baby. Next morning the little boy came across from the neighbouring garden and spent the whole day with me, as though we had always been old friends. His parents were especially astonished because he was a rather nervous child and they had never before known him do anything like it. But, when we consider that the appearance of a new rival

IDENTIFICATION

was far from being an agreeable event in the child's life, we shall understand his bold attempt at flight.

Another observation showed me that 'going for a walk by oneself' means for a child 'going away from Mummy'. A six-year-old boy went into the street by himself for the first time because he was angry with his mother for refusing him something he wanted. A few weeks later a strange little episode occurred in connection with the same child, who in the meantime had gone for a number of short walks by himself without any particular excitement. As he was going out, his mother saw him out of the window and called out a friendly word to him. The little boy stopped, answered, made a lot of nonsensical remarks, danced about impatiently where he was standing, and finally shouted angrily: 'I want to go off now!' 'Well, go off then!' said the mother. To which he replied: 'But I can't so long as I see you!' And it was not until his mother had gone away from the window that he was able to start for his walk.

The fact that towards the beginning of school age parents are thrown into the background by no means implies any diminution of their influence upon the development of a child's character. Physical, mental and social ties continue to bind him to his parents and so it is that the 'mental emigration' that I have just mentioned takes place for the most part along paths prescribed or sanctioned by the parents (as, for instance, when a child is sent to school). This means that the climax of the Œdipus complex is succeeded by the period of educability. The stormy and contradictory feelings are replaced by identification with the parents. We know from what has gone before that identification disposes

IDENTIFICATION

of an aggressive, rebellious feeling and does so by making a powerful external impression into a part of our own ego. That is precisely what a child does with commands and prohibitions which he is obliged to obey, so that he ends by being able to believe that he is following his own will. This procedure can easily be observed in quite small children. A child who cries bitterly if an attempt is made to carry him forcibly out of the room will calm down if he is given an opportunity of going out 'of his own accord'. It is possible in this way to get most children to want things that are the exact opposite of what they wanted originally. The protest which children raise against orders comes clearly to light in a number of very common childish habits. For instance, everyone knows that children are more inclined to obey if we tell them to do the opposite of what we want. Indeed, they will often say straight out: 'Tell me not to do it and I'll do it'.[1] The meaning is much the same, too, when a child amuses himself by using words in the sense opposite to their real one and says 'yes' instead of 'no', etc.

All these games are in reality attempts at preserving self-esteem in the face of superior power; and it becomes clear from this that giving way is painful to a child, irrespective of what it is that he is ordered to do. He even dislikes doing under orders something that he would otherwise be glad to do. This violent protest is in the end the cause of the child's defeat. Since his narcissism is incapable of tolerating a com-

[1] Among the North American Indian tribes there used to be societies whose members were young warriors who, according to their rules, always did the opposite of what they were told. During a battle, for instance, if someone called out to them 'Retire!', they would advance even if it meant certain death.

IDENTIFICATION

mand, he becomes prepared at last, rather than obey, to will the same thing that the adults require him to do. The child who gets out of the room 'of his own accord' is giving up his own will for the sake of preserving a fictitious 'free will'.

The outcome of the struggle round an individual's narcissism is one of the most important events of his development. As a result of identification with the various commands and prohibitions, his ego undergoes a decisive transformation. Since obedience takes place not through understanding but through identification, the command becomes a part of the child's ego, which he defends henceforward just as much as his own will. This is the explanation of the remarkable, rigid conservatism with which a child clings to regulations when he has once accepted them. To be sure, we must not forget at this point that, just as repression is unable to destroy the instinct from which a forbidden wish arises, so identification with the will of the adults does not do away with the wishes that are in contradiction to that will. The consequence is a splitting of the ego into two parts, of which one is the vehicle of the original instinctual wishes while the other is the vehicle of the wishes that have been incorporated by means of identification. This second, transformed part of the ego is called by Freud the 'super-ego'. The super-ego behaves towards the instinctual ego precisely as a child's educators originally behaved to the child. The child feels the educatory origin of the super-ego as his conscience. Yet conscience, however disagreeable it may be upon occasion, is no longer an external but an internal compulsion, in obeying which the child can feel as though he were acting in accordance with a wish of his own. We may often observe that it is

IDENTIFICATION

precisely the most self-willed children who become the most conscientious. Those children who can least tolerate punishment are inclined to anticipate it with remorse or even with self-punishment. In such a case a child is behaving like a hero who, rather than fall into the hands of his enemies, puts an end to his own life or who (as we know from historical instances), if he is to be executed, will not let himself be bound, but ascends the scaffold 'free' and as though the decision to do so were his own. In moments of critical danger adults are themselves in the same situation as a child in relation to his parents: in both cases the sense of complete surrender leads to similar measures of defence.

Some people will certainly think it exaggerated to compare a child who is undergoing his education with a man in mortal danger. Nevertheless, from the point of view of the instinctual ego, the comparison comes very close to reality. The coming into existence of the super-ego can be regarded as a sentence of death upon the primitive life of the instincts. We can see this most clearly in children's behaviour. In any nursery a child who is asked who did this or that forbidden act may be heard answering that *he* was not the guilty one but some other, naughtier person. This other person is often given a name and becomes a permanent guest in the nursery. Many suppose that this is merely a lie and that the child simply wants to deny his misdemeanour for fear of being punished. But there is something in the form taken by the denial that catches our attention. The child does not deny the misdemeanour but only that it was he who committed it. He is trying to regard the part of his mind that has become disagreeable to him owing to the

IDENTIFICATION

threats (or merely prohibitions) of his educators as something alien and outside himself. And he is perfectly ready to join with the adults in jeering at this naughty other person or in beating him or even in destroying him. Of course we also learn from time to time that this other person is very powerful and clever, so that it is not so easy to get rid of him. But if on an occasion like this we try to make it clear to the child that this naughty other person is himself, then the understanding between us breaks down and violent protests ensue. The child's behaviour in this connection is exactly like his behaviour towards physical pains: he attempts by means of projection to get rid of the disturbing portion of his ego.

Rasmussen, in his *Child Psychology*, writes: 'At the age of 4 years and 1 month Ruth used occasionally to vomit a little after her midday meal. I corrected her and told her it was not nice. By way of excuse Ruth remarked: "Yes, but *I* didn't do it; I didn't want to, but my tummy did it".—A fortnight later she wanted to be naughty and began to stamp her foot. But she soon stopped, stamped once more very gently and said: "One of my legs is rather naughty".' In the second of these examples the splitting of the ego takes place before our very eyes. The first angry stamping still shows the individual undivided: then comes the recollection of the prohibition and the repudiation of the naughty portion of the ego.

Thus in the splitting of the ego two forces play a part, forces which are closely interrelated but which are clearly to be distinguished: one of these is identification with the behaviour of the environment and the other is projection

IDENTIFICATION

of the portion of the ego which has become disagreeable precisely owing to that identification. It is probably only later, in connection with the development of the sense of reality, that there sets in repression—that is, a complete elimination from consciousness—of the affects and wishes which were in the first instance projected. For to begin with a child makes no distinction between his world of phantasy and reality. At that stage of development he is quite content with the fiction that the guilty foot does not belong to him. It is not until this notion becomes untenable that he is obliged to have recourse to repression. For something of which I know nothing can surely not be 'I': even the grown-ups must see that. Accordingly, it would be a necessary precondition of repression that we should have identified ourselves with the adult idea of reality.

The process of super-ego formation discovered by Freud, which I have been so far discussing, is in general represented as a method of adaptation to the prohibitions and commands of the environment. That, however, is only one side of this immensely important psychological phenomenon. Ferenczi's experiences in adult analyses, and particularly in character analyses, show that super-ego formation, though originally a form of adaptation to external reality, can none the less become an obstacle to subsequent adaptations. According to Ferenczi, the splitting of the ego as a result of identification with a prohibition involves serious damage to the ego. The first sign that a splitting of the ego is setting in is a child's protest against the assumption that he himself is 'the guilty person'. The disadvantage of this method of dealing with the situation is obvious. It is true that it may lead to the

IDENTIFICATION

child (taking the last example) no longer stamping her foot; but we can no longer discuss with the child *why* she stamped. Henceforward she will always put us off by saying that it was her foot and not she herself that was 'naughty'. The fact that the 'why' remained hidden in Rasmussen's instance as well is shown by the typical way in which the account of the whole episode is worded: 'one day she wanted to be naughty'. The educators lay the stress upon the rule of conduct: 'you must not stamp your foot at your parents'. Any impulses that cause the emergence of a wish to stamp are therefore to be dreaded, and the child will have nothing to do with them. In this way, however, after the super-ego formation has been effected, both parts of the ego cease to be susceptible to influence: one because it is split off and no longer recognized as a portion of our self, and the other, which has already been made rigid by identification with the prohibition, because it only admits of a strictly circumscribed method of behaviour. Any lifting of the rigid regulation is guarded against by the anxiety which made the identification (the splitting of the ego) necessary. Thus we see that every adaptation by means of identification is at the same time a limitation upon the free and elastic capacity for adaptation which rests upon an understanding judgment of the situation. In place of that capacity we only too often find a rigid, automatic character which, though it is a product of practical acts of adaptation, can nevertheless find itself in gross conflict with the demands of reality.[1] In what

---

[1] The removal of the splitting of the ego by recollecting its causative experiences can enable a person to submit his automatisms to conscious control. Such conscious control and the accompanying reduction of

IDENTIFICATION

follows I shall return to the consideration of how educational methods can be adapted so as to reduce to a minimum the development of automatisms of character.

This discussion must inevitably raise the question of how the part played by identification can be reconciled with the domination of the pleasure principle in mental life. It is true that, as we have seen, identification always operates in the interest of narcissism and does what it can to defend narcissism; yet it may well seem that the price paid for that defence is far too high. The child takes over the adults' desires and tastes and makes them his own; following their example, he is ready to condemn what has previously been pleasurable to him and ultimately he goes so far as to remove the forbidden feelings and thoughts entirely from his consciousness.

Children will not infrequently tell us how hard it is for them to fulfil these requirements. A little girl of seven once said to me: 'I'm not allowed to do anything nice and I have to do everything nasty'. And here is the heart-rending complaint made to his mother by a six-year-old boy: 'I'd no idea when I was born that I should have such a bad time'. When his mother asked him in astonishment what had happened to him that was so terrible, he enumerated all those apparently trivial prohibitions and restrictions which *we* scarcely notice but which embitter a child's life.

And in this connection we must not forget that complaints of this kind are only made by children who are in a relatively

anxiety is of course not the same thing as a reduction of the inhibitions of instinct that are necessary to civilization. What happens is simply that anxiety is replaced as the basis for the restriction of instinct by love and reason.

IDENTIFICATION

good state, that is to say, who retain some degree of freedom of thought. The most tactful education cannot protect a child from the sufferings necessarily involved in the process of putting a rein upon the instincts—partly because education begins at an age at which it is too early for us to be able to count on understanding and partly because the measures in question are not always of a kind where understanding is possible. For the requirements imposed upon small children are to a great extent a matter of convention and the only ground for obeying them is fear of losing the parents' love. Yet it follows from the narcissistic nature of young children that the love which they receive from their environment, essential though it is to them, cannot compensate them for the loss of their primitive instinctual gratifications. A child depends upon us to a high degree, but he does not love us enough to be able to make so great a sacrifice for our sake. That is to say, we can only force him to make the renunciation, without being in a position to offer him a full compensation for it. But against all this there is the fact that a human being is only able to make a renunciation in return for some substitute gratification, which, indeed, follows from our inability to extinguish the instincts by any defensive measures. But it is in the very nature of an instinct to strive to find its way by some path or other to its inevitable discharge. The question thus arises in what manner a child gratifies the instincts with which, on the basis of his identification with his educators, he has repudiated any kind of association.

When I was speaking of the education of the instincts, I mentioned that the various inhibitions divert an instinct

IDENTIFICATION

from its original direction. It is true, of course, that a diversion of this kind is not possible in the case of every instinct: for instance, hunger can only be satisfied by eating. Susceptibility to diversion is primarily a quality of the sexual instincts. This peculiarity, coupled with identificatory thinking, affords them an almost unlimited possibility of making their way through. And in this, the opportunities for gratification that are offered by identification with adults play a particularly important part, since they facilitate considerably a child's social adaptation.

At a first glance this assertion may seem strange: for identification with his elders brings a child little else than a restriction of his instincts. But the apparent contradiction can be explained by an example. Let us take an event that occurs in the life of every child. Uncle Doctor arrives and looks down the child's throat with a spoon. On the first such occasion most children react violently against the assault and make it absolutely clear that the whole thing is very far indeed from pleasing them. But, strange to say, instead of forgetting the unpleasant business as quickly as possible, they almost without exception begin soon afterwards to play at doctor. Thus the child behaves after the doctor's visit just as he does after parting from an object that he likes. (Cf. the example of the dog on page 100.) This is all the more peculiar because, according to what we have hitherto found, a child identifies himself with an absent object in order to replace it and so get rid of his longing for it. But children do not long for the doctor: so what can be the meaning of the identification here? The child dislikes what the doctor does to him but he is compelled to submit to it. Then, afterwards,

IDENTIFICATION

the child becomes the doctor, looks down everyone's throat, applies compresses, gives medicine, and so on. Thus he does actively what he suffered passively. We know how much it injures a child's narcissism if he is obliged to put up with something against his will. By means of the identification, he brings about the interchange of rôles which he so much desires. Moreover, in playing at doctor the child is able to express his anger. This is shown by the fact that the whole procedure is as a rule repeated in the game in a more merciless fashion than the child himself actually experienced. We find the same thing happen when children play at Mummy and Daddy or at School. Children who have never been hit will beat their dolls black and blue for the sort of offences that they themselves commit. The splitting of the ego, which I spoke of above, makes it possible for a child to abreact his aggressiveness not only upon his dolls or upon other objects but also upon himself. The severity towards our own self which we call conscience is indeed nothing but a turning back of our sadism upon our own ego.

We have already discussed the narcissistic pleasure which a child obtains from its identification with a command. To this we may now add that by falling in with the command the child becomes more like the adult and that anything that diminishes the gap between the two of them soothes the injury suffered by the child's narcissism. In order to be like adults, children will put up with the boredom of being good, will consent to dress in uncomfortable clothes—in short, will think anything in the world desirable merely because it forms part of the adults' system of life. This narcissistic advantage still further increases the conservative way in

IDENTIFICATION

which, as I have already remarked, a child clings to a command when once he has obeyed it. Incidentally, this conservatism is also a good method by which to abreact his aggressiveness. In every nursery we can see the way in which from time to time the adults become the slaves of their own commands. There is no one more critical than a child: he perceives the slightest inconsistency in his parents' behaviour and makes them pay for it.

For instance, a little boy was promised by his father that he would take him for a walk on Sunday. Some visitors came, however, and the promise was forgotten. In the middle of lunch the child suddenly declared in deadly serious tones: 'Daddy tells lies too!' Since obedience (in the present instance the love of truth) is not the result of understanding but of identification, the child knows neither compromise nor consideration. So it can come about that by means of identification a code of laws is established in the child, which brings him into a growing opposition to his own parents and that he turns against his parents the commands which he took over from them.

A good example of this is offered by daughters. We may often find that, if a daughter who has been brought up on extremely moral lines discovers that her mother is in fact living in sexual relations with a man, she will either feel a profound contempt for her or pity her as a poor, weak woman who is compelled to humiliate herself. For the severe daughter, by identification with her educative prohibitions, has long ago blotted out of her mind the fact that she herself once had longings for a sexual life and that all her wishes took the direction of wanting, like her mummy, to be loved

IDENTIFICATION

by her daddy, to have children and to feed them. Along with all the rest of the commands, she has obeyed the one which told her that a girl must not have such thoughts; but her old grudge reappears in the severity with which she now condemns her mother. In this highly typical case the mother's behaviour intensifies the child's impulse to identify herself with her commands instead of loving and comprehending. Love is made more difficult by the fact that the mother permits herself what she forbids to the child; and comprehension is wrecked by the contradictory discovery that an adult is quite free to do what in a child is regarded as a piece of naughtiness or even as a sin.

The educational methods adopted determine whether a child identifies itself with the command or with the real parents. In either case the result may be an estrangement between parents and children. If the education is strict, then the child (as in the previous example) will identify himself with the commands and, from the height of his superior self-control, will look down with contemptuous condemnation upon his parents and the whole of adult society. If the pressure of education is less severe, then the child will identify himself with the parents, will do what they do and will come into conflict with the prohibitions and commands which will be constantly insisted upon—even though unsuccessfully—by his wider environment. In that case it will be made impossible for the child to be 'good'. He does everything like his parents and none the less is met with nothing but reproofs. The uncertainty in which such a child finds himself makes love for his parents no less difficult than in a straightforward character formation based upon identifica-

IDENTIFICATION

tion. Here, too, the final result will be estrangement. A person who has remained under the sway of his instincts will come into conflict with his parents, who preach morality but have given him neither the strength for self-control nor a true freedom.

In this way, then, it comes about that identification itself may in the long run separate children from their parents. The most effective counter-measure is that, in educating a child, we should seek from the very first to work as much as possible upon his reason—in other words, to replace identification, so far as we possibly can, by understanding. This can be achieved in a variety of ways. In the first place, we must give up any attempt at producing records in the direction of early training. For what we gain by that means in rapid adaptation we lose in flexibility of thought. Thus many things which a child of one or two can only accomplish by means of identification can without too much trouble be made intelligible to a child of three or four. Of course we must not imagine that by measures of this kind we can get rid of identification altogether. To begin with, it sets in at a stage long before explanations of any sort are possible, and, in the second place, as we are already aware 'understanding' and 'explaining' are also based upon identification. Nevertheless, we can avoid producing too great a rigidity in identification, too gross a subjugation of the child's ego. If he is not obliged to condemn his own wish in addition to obeying the educatory command, much less of his aggressiveness towards his parents will be worked into the identification.

Another effective way in which it is possible to avoid blind adaptation based upon identification lies in adults being ready openly to admit, even to quite small children, any occasional mistakes of their own.[1] We mean, of course, such mistakes as the child himself might make and can himself as a rule detect. Admitting a mistake encourages him to use his powers of criticism and to dare to think for himself. It is instructive to watch a child when a mistake or a piece of ignorance has been admitted to him by his parents. On the one hand he is delighted by the event since it brings him closer to them, but on the other hand he protests against it and insists that they should not make mistakes but should remain omniscient and omnipotent. For if parents too can make mistakes, there is a risk of losing the substitute gratification which the child has tried to achieve by means of identification. A child begins by regarding himself as omnipotent; then, when he is compelled to obey a command, he abandons this omnipotence, but at the same time attributes it to his parents whom, by means of identification, he seeks to resemble.

Numbers of children's sayings prove that in their phantasy nothing is impossible to their parents. Here is one example out of many. A girl of six was refused something she wanted on the ground that her father had no money. The child: 'Then, why don't you make some, Daddy?' The father: 'Only the King can do that'. The child (greatly disappointed): 'But aren't you a King?' The following episode shows how

[1] This way of behaving to children agrees precisely with Ferenczi's advice upon the behaviour of analysts in character analyses. He recommends the admission by the analyst of any occasional slips or errors that he may make as being one of the most valuable helps in the difficult work of demolishing what has become an automatic method of behaving on the part of the patient.

deeply a child's narcissism is injured when it turns out that someone (his father, for instance) with whom he has identified himself is not the most important person in the world. The father was mountaineering, and the little boy heard on this occasion that someone else and not his father was acting as leader. He found the fact quite incredible and it was hardly possible to make him understand that his father was not always first—the one position that he himself wanted to occupy.

What children so often sigh for—'when I'm grown up'—means, as we all know, 'when I can do everything I want to'. Thus identification is a means by which they seek to recapture their old position of autocracy; and this hope is increased by parents who, while being strict with their children, allow themselves every sort of indulgence. Most parents believe that they are educating their children for the tasks of life by exacting unquestioning obedience and limitless faith from them. But the facts are just the other way, and children are brought into closer contact with reality if they learn that even their parents are neither omnipotent nor infallible.

By way of summary, it may be said that identification never fails to reveal itself as a direct derivative of narcissism. Even though it sometimes looks as though it were a means towards doing without something and making an adaptation, it turns out in the end that it is clinging obstinately to its original aim, the defence of narcissism. In contrast to narcissism, love and understanding are the two factors by whose help we enter into a true relation with reality. From this it follows that in education we must attach the greatest

IDENTIFICATION

importance to these two motive forces. Capacity to love and understanding (or reason) are the two genuine weapons for the conquest of the external world. For, while through identification we yield to external force by way of a kind of mimicry, love and reason enable us to influence the external world in the direction of our wishes.

Conclusion

THE CHILD'S LIBERATION

I WELL remember the first time that I heard of an instance of the following kind. A psycho-analyst told me how a mother came to him with her small daughter, whom she wanted him to treat on account of various neurotic symptoms. Since his practice did not include the treatment of children, and it was at once apparent that the mother was herself neurotic and must thus have contributed to her child's condition, he advised her to undergo analysis herself. The mother agreed, and, as the physician had expected, her own cure had the further result of curing her daughter. Although in this case the child's neurosis might readily have been attributed to heredity, the fact emerges that the improvement of an important part of the child's environment, namely the mother, led also to the establishment of a normal, healthy equilibrium in the child.

This is only an instance from among the many testimonies available from psycho-analytical experience to the hypothesis that—extreme cases apart—in the origin of neurosis the constitutional factor, predisposition, plays generally the smaller part, and the environment the predominant one. Even the provoking causes of such an illness (traumas) derive their meaning and importance from the total situation in which the child encounters them. The same event may in one environment be endured by a child without ill effects, while in another it is the last drop which makes the full cup overflow. The kind of environment, the tone prevailing in the family, the parents' characters, the general treatment meted out to the child, and especially the proportion of things forbidden to things allowed—all these things play a decisive part. Parents, therefore, exercise a prodigious power over individual destinies; it is they who bear responsibility, in the last resort, for the good or bad character, the sound or defective development of their children. That is, they ought to bear the responsibility if only they were conscious of their power.

But parents are aware only of their conscious processes, and are vouchsafed no clear view of the concealed ways in which their whole personality, their ways of life, their customs, etc., influence their child. Thus many a son, who feels himself estranged and different from his father, has no idea that he himself has developed on that father's pattern; and how few parents see that, in spite of all their efforts, it is *their own faults* that are reproduced in their children. If they do see this, they are far more ready to invoke heredity than the much simpler explanation, that what they themselves *are* influences the child as greatly as, or even more greatly than, what they merely say.

THE CHILD'S LIBERATION

It is only this ignorance as to what is involved that clears the educator of the real charge of responsibility, and makes it inappropriate for us even to raise the question of blame. The time in which we have known anything worth mentioning about the veiled processes of human development is comparatively short—not long enough, certainly, to enable us to pass final judgment in every case. It is not indiscriminate accusations, but patient collection of knowledge from experience that should concern us. We have to recognize that more understanding and deeper insight into the real problems presented by particular circumstances are essential for any truly successful work in education.

But here it may well be objected that even if all that psycho-analysis has established as to the significance of earliest childhood experiences is true, all parents can hardly be expected to be trained psychologists. Although this sounds a daunting implication, I do not believe it need be regarded as impossible. One need only substitute 'natural' for 'trained'. In consequence of the far-reaching repression made necessary by modern education we have lost a valuable part of natural psychological sensitivity, which people more untaught but less 'repressed' have often retained.

Thus it is not so much the acquisition of yet more knowledge which is required of educators, as the regaining of what has been forgotten. *The main need for an understanding upbringing is, basically, nothing else but the recollection of what we all knew as children.* We know how difficult this recollection is, yet it is by no means impossible. But—it may further be objected—is this knowledge so necessary? We have seen that the limitation of instincts is a necessary concomitant of civilization;

if we have to perform this sacrifice, perhaps it is better accomplished unconsciously than consciously. One chooses an anaesthetic rather than conscious endurance of pain.

Yet we must note that anaesthesia, too, may have its real dangers. One might have a number of sound teeth extracted, without the possibility of protesting against what was happening. One result, certainly unintended, of our methods of upbringing is a general blunting (well comparable to anaesthesia) of our self-knowledge. The memory of our losses and renunciations in childhood is a thing to be forgotten and buried as quickly and completely as possible, and resentment at our sufferings is usually transposed into the formula 'what I bore, you can bear too'. So one generation avenges itself on the next for the ruin of its childhood happiness.

This childhood happiness and, in consequence, general human happiness, has in our civilization become contracted to an alarming degree. Plaints about children's sufferings fill the air. Novels, which used to deal mostly with the vicissitudes of lovers, are now largely preoccupied with childhood, which is usually depicted as a period of griefs and terrors. And this just at a time when the problem of pedagogics has come to the forefront, and when so much interest is being taken in the many new suggestions in the fields of teaching and child-guidance for making children's lives happier and easier.

I am of opinion that the ever-increasing preoccupation with pedagogic problems is itself a consequence of the worsening which has become apparent to us in our children's situation. This worsening is psychical in nature, and applies in the same way to working-class children, exposed to all sorts of hazards, as to the more sheltered classes. Modern urban civilization has brought about changes in the child's environment, which intensify the difficulties of surmounting the obstacles in the path of human development. The most significant signs of this modification are the greater need, for the city-child, of care and protection from its parents, and the greater tension between instinct and the demands of morality and propriety. We may add as a third important factor, that together with the greater (i.e. longer lasting) dependence of our children there arises the need, previously almost unheard-of, that when their education is completed they should become so far as possible independent of their parents, in material matters as well as those of the mind. In earlier days the whole way of life, the younger generation's occupation, even its home, was taken over unchanged from the previous one, and the individual was only obliged to exchange the first childish love-object for another, otherwise being able to keep the whole familiar environment unchanged; but the young today, in our urbanized civilization, must in just these respects accustom themselves to homelessness. The lot which earlier befell only exceptional individuals, reformers, discoverers, or adventurers, today must be sustained by us all.

Let us look at what this change in the general conditions of our lives signifies from the psychical aspect. The urban child's increased need of protection, and dependence, means in the first place that the general difficulties of development, which may almost be termed biological, and which we have described as the Œdipus and castration complexes, are thrown into much sharper relief. The parents become in reality the only stable points in our children's lives. Urban man is a homeless wanderer. He is attached to no birthplace, that is, no settled home to which his child may transfer a part of its feelings, and spends his life in a constantly changing environment. Yet while the primitive nomads simply carry their children on their backs, and remain within a comparatively permanent group, our children are entrusted to strangers (nurses, neighbours, baby sitters, employees) who through circumstances are always apt to forsake them, and the sole certain figures, the parents, transform themselves into remote objects of longing.

For the town child, there is together with a lesser stability in environment a lesser freedom in instinctual activity. While the country child has, with its greater scope for movement, greater opportunity for satisfying its instincts with impunity, the town child, especially when brought up in comfortable circumstances, is always under the observing eyes of adults. The child confined to the four walls of its parents' home feels as though on an island in a strange and hostile world, with whose dangers it must all too soon become familiar. One of the most important factors in the hostile and distrustful attitude which is interposed between us and the world around us is precisely our proudest acquisition of civilization—hygiene. Strangers who want to pet or kiss a child are promptly repulsed. The way in which the world appears to a well brought up child in such circumstances is shown by the response of a little girl of four, who when asked what she came across in the public playground replied 'Germs!'

It is in such conditions that 'the nursery' has arisen as really a new phenomenon. It is a small world, with fear and mystery walling off its surroundings; it affords its child-inhabitants no opportunity of making comparisons with the world outside, and every event within it seems just on this account unique and is invested with heightened significance. The result is a *sultry atmosphere in the nursery, arising from fear of the world outside and unappeased longing for closer intimacy with the parents.* This longing, strangely enough, is still more intensified by the actual limitations of living-space imposed on modern families, for the many deceptions and mysteries which consequently surround children make a true intimate life the more impossible. The child, to get light on the secrets surrounding it, becomes an eavesdropper and spy, and the objects of its curiosity are inevitably the only persons close to it—yet so remote—the parents. And fear of the world outside intensifies in turn the anxiety felt in relation to the parents. Children cling to them as their only support, and any disunity or quarrels between the parents, their anger, sufferings, or illness, are felt by the children as undermining the whole basis of their existence. It is in this general climate of heightened anxiety, longings, and curiosity, that education must nowadays proceed.

Clearly in such circumstances it is no easy task to avoid contributing by education that 'too much of a good thing' whereby a child's mental balance, already threatened, may be upset. Education is no mathematical problem, admitting of only one solution every time, but may far better be compared to a campaign in diplomacy which must always be conducted with due regard for the various forces at work in the current situation. The same measures, in upbringing and education, which in one case come near enough to

THE CHILD'S LIBERATION

achieving what is wanted, may in another do great harm. The same words, according to the tone in which they are spoken, may as we know have opposite effects.

A problem not easily answered arises when, for example, one is told how unaccountable it is that this or that child should show such a resentful disposition, when in fact it has never been struck, never had a hard word, always has everything it wants, and so on. It is in fact the case that often a piece of scolding, an open display of impatience or lost temper on the part of the adults, may be less distressing for a child than the constant moral pressure which turns many nurseries with an apparently friendly atmosphere into true torture chambers.

Examples may make the matter clearer. A little girl of about nine enthusiastically began something she intended to say with the words 'I want. . . .' The governess interrupted her with 'Children do not say, *I want*'. This went on over and over again, the governess never getting angry but calmly and patiently repeating her injunction—until the child's enthusiasm vanished, and in the end she never managed to say what she had actually 'wanted'.[1]

Another child, a little boy of five, wanted very much to take some grapes that were on the table before him. The governess refused permission with the following gently reproachful words 'How can you vex me so?' The child's eyes filled with tears. In this case we see that an especially

---

[1] The 'I want', though less forceful than the German 'ich will', is a fair English equivalent. I well remember being told not to say it, and on my temerariously asking what I *could* say, being told 'Not "*I want*", dear, "I *should like*"—but try not to begin your sentences with "I"!' (*Translator*.)

sensitive conscience has been successfully inculcated, but whether the child then or later is the happier for it may indeed be doubted. The 'meekness' of the governess is properly speaking a lie. She is by no means meek and kind, but so strict and intolerant that this small impropriety (grapes at the beginning of dinner instead of the end) is felt by her as a major lapse. And the child's tears which were welcomed as repentance are in truth the tears of suppressed rage. An educator who is never 'cross' over a child's naughtiness, only 'deeply hurt' or 'greatly surprised', can inflict the most effective suffering. Plaints and tears are no use, only complete subjection by repression of the child's own ego. Naturally this can only occur in our nurseries, where the possibility of any kind of 'running away' is excluded. In a simpler society, with more freedom of movement, the same educational tormentor might be seen as a harmless or even comical nonentity, at whom the child might turn up its nose.

But now we must ask, what possibility is there of making the nursery a tolerable place? The nursery (and with it one must include for present purposes the kindergarten and school) is made necessary, and conditioned, by the lengthy period of development which is required for civilized children in order that they may sustain the struggle for existence. The only way which can be generally recommended to help children over the disadvantages of this long period of preparation is—*honesty*. And by honesty I mean, *honesty of adults towards themselves and towards children*. After all that has been said above about the difficulties of self-knowledge—for that indeed means honesty towards oneself—no one will suppose that this is hollow advice. It means

THE CHILD'S LIBERATION

that through knowledge of our own feelings, through awareness of our own conflicts of childhood, we can come to a sound appreciation of our children's situation. So, and only so, we may avert the risk that because of our unawareness, acquired through repression, we treat the small child almost as an automatic doll, with no opinion of its own, no self-originating feelings and wishes. So we shall learn *to behave towards children with as much consideration as towards adults*. We shall encourage them to express their thoughts as freely as possible, and we shall explain the reasons for the prohibitions and restrictions that we find necessary. We shall acknowledge that children are excellent observers and acute critics, and we shall refrain from trying to put them off with unnecessary deceptions. I once heard a girl of six say to her mother, who was asserting that she was simply obliged to go away, 'Why do you always say you *have* to go, why don't you say you *want* to?' With this the child showed not only that she saw through her mother's attitude, but that the truth might safely have been told her.

Honesty on the part of the parents by no means implies spoiling of the children. I am not saying that, because the child might have liked her mother to stay at home, the mother ought to have done so. And the child would not have minded less being left alone, whatever reason was given. The advantage of honesty lies in another direction. It enables the child to feel that it *shares the grown-ups' feelings*—that they are the same. The grown-ups are brought closer to the child who learns that they, like it, can only partly give free rein to their wishes, and partly must obey necessity. Fellow-feeling with grown-ups is a very rare thing in children. As a

THE CHILD'S LIBERATION

rule a child only discovers when he or she grows up—and even then not always—that the parents are not mere educating automata and doers of duty, but 'people'. The failure in comprehension lies, not in the child's lack of feeling, but in the kind of education which affords the child no opportunity of getting to know the real natures of the educators. Many of the latter regard it as unfitting, impertinent, and derogatory to themselves, if a child comes to ascribe to them the same feelings, weaknesses and passions as its own. The consequences of this educational outlook are the coldness and hardness so often displayed by the young towards the older generation.

Just as unnecessary as the concealment of our feelings is the concealment of the *real dangers and misfortunes* to which children like all mankind are exposed. In the very nursery where all mention of such things as illness, death, worry, and ill-fortune is avoided—where when someone dies, they say he has gone away, and so on—there broods the figure of the bogey-man, who will come to fetch the child who is naughty. The child forbidden to lean out of the window, for example, is not told that it may kill itself if it falls, but that the policeman or some other alarming figure will come after it. To be told the truth about real dangers gets a child gradually into the way of being able to take care of itself; but the threat of some omnipresent inescapable bogey, coupled with the constant warding-off of dangers which are not explained, tends to rob the child of the ability and courage to attain true freedom. If one tries to save a child from knowledge of the harsher side of life it may come to believe that if a person is only well-behaved and tractable,

THE CHILD'S LIBERATION

all ills will be averted. This belief enormously enhances the power of the parents, yet just on this account it happens that experiences which give it the lie have serious traumatic effects. Death or illness in the family may throw the child into most pitiable anxiety and insecurity. Either it must doubt the parents' power, and then there is no security left in the world; or it may cling to its belief, and feel the more terrified of its parents who mete out such cruel punishments. Simple, truthful explanations certainly disclose to children the limitations on parents' power, but the real-life anxiety which they arouse never compares with the boundless terror of the child who in its ignorance sees evil everywhere.

We conclude therefore: *honesty is the way to inner liberation of the child*, and that of the grown-ups with it—in spite of the confined nursery world, and the long period of dependence, in which the apprenticeship years must be spent. We have seen what a bad expedient it is to try to recompense ourselves for the trouble of the slow process of education by inciting a greater attachment to ourselves on the child's part. Such an attachment may degenerate into fear of life, inner lack of independence, an impoverishment of emotion. We shall not, by such means, bring up more affectionate children—only less happy and less healthy adults. We have to learn that the chief aim of education is *emancipation from the nursery*. True education, upbringing, can be nothing else than the setting forth from the nursery, and—however painful this may be for us—from the parents. It is only those parents who open this road—hard enough, as it is, for the children—who may hope to keep their child in later years, not indeed as a submissive slave, but as an equal friend.

Appendix

FUNDAMENTALS OF OUR EDUCATION[1]

WE all recognize the significance of man's long childhood, which we regard as the biological basis of the Œdipus complex and the development of the super-ego. On this occasion I turn to consider that secondary prolongation of childhood which characterizes our own civilization. I mean, by this, the prolongation of the preparatory period required for the attainment of social maturity. Undoubtedly there is a very close connection between this prolonged childhood and the fact that the rôle of work in our way of living has become that of a lifelong and systematic effort. In another paper, dealing with 'prohibition and concession in upbringing', I have made the point that civilized man's life requires, from earliest childhood, a systematic training in the toleration of stresses and tensions. This, beginning in infancy with regulated

[1] Contribution to a symposium on 'Revision of Psycho-analytical Pedagogy', Budapest 1937.

feeding-times, may also be regarded as a perpetual succession of small traumas tending to the detachment of the child from its mother—a series of experiences destined to befall the child, from the very beginning, with fairly regular persistence.

The educational problem arises here from the contradiction between these measures, aimed in early childhood at the loosening of the tie with the mother, and the moral condemnation of the child's turning away from the parents in the comparatively prolonged period of its dependence in both early and later youth. Thus, what is sought after in the earliest upbringing has to be undone, as it were, in later childhood.

A comparison with primitive social conditions will bring this out more clearly. (I must explain, however, that I use the term in a somewhat summary, or rather schematic, sense, and the conditions to which I refer, while prevailing in a number of primitive societies, may be entirely different among other similar peoples.)

After a comparatively long infancy, during which the child's existence is formally regarded as being one with its mother's, the boy, either when he is about seven or at any later time till puberty, is with more or less ceremonial detached from her. Thus one of the main duties observed by these societies towards their growing children is to intervene between mother and child in order to facilitate emancipation from the mothers—whether the intervention is mild or so firm that it amounts to cruelty, it does further that process. From a certain stage onwards, a boy should not and may not show affection towards his mother.

FUNDAMENTALS OF OUR EDUCATION

With us, on the other hand, after an infancy which is comparatively short, and regulated by education, comes the moral requirement of love for the mother, extending well beyond puberty and, strictly speaking, for a lifetime. A main problem for adult society *vis-à-vis* adolescence is, how to maintain the love and attachment even throughout this time of storm and stress, without diminishing the educability of youth. For primitives, puberty is a happening of the greatest importance, in which the whole society participates, and which brings about an entirely new orientation of youthful interests and attachments. For civilized society, it is something which should in decency be hardly noticed; from the educative aspect it is usually seen as a very unwelcome disturbance, something to which no place can be allotted in the proper programme of life. Whilst puberty in primitive society is reciprocally related with the environment, in civilized life it is eminently an inner experience. All the first ties of childhood subsist and must be maintained; the task of detachment falls to the child itself, to be accomplished under the pressure of guilt.

We know that, wherever a moral verdict governs man's attitude, an over-compensation is present. About the third or fourth year of life the first, instinctual, tie between mother and child is gradually dissolved. In the child, separative tendencies become active with the passing of the Œdipus complex. This I have termed 'mental emigration'; Hermann regards it as the manifestation of an instinct which forms the counterpart of the instinct to cling. At about the same time the mother's 'parental erotism', as Ferenczi terms it, tends to turn towards the next child. Through over-compensation of both these tendencies to detachment the mutual bond between mother and child is secondarily, and indefinitely, prolonged, and the result is an almost insoluble ambivalence.

The primitive child has only to struggle with the guilty feelings arising from the Œdipus complex; our children are additionally oppressed by the guilt of later childhood, when in the face of all usage and tradition they feel the impulse to separate from their mother.

To sum up, we may express the dual orientation of our system as follows:

1. In earliest childhood the manifestations both of instinctual motherhood and of the infant's instinct to cling are inhibited;

2. In later childhood, in contrast, comes the inhibition of the mutual tendencies to detachment. Here, too, belongs the paralysis of the instinctual energies, emerging in puberty, that strive towards the attainment of maturity.

Two of the conspicuous psychological characteristics of our civilization seem to me to follow from these facts. The one is common knowledge, the other has been elicited mainly by psycho-analytical research. They are:

1. The importance, for our culture, acquired by *individuality*;

2. The *increased fear of loss of love*, into which, as it seems to me, the original castration-anxiety practically merges. It is not the father's might, but the mother's turning away, that is most deeply dreaded. In my opinion this explains the relative impotence which, as Freud maintains, characterizes our civilization. The father can be defeated, but the mother remains for ever unattainable.

Although the heightened fear of loss of love is a pathological phenomenon, the increased significance of individuality seems to constitute a way out of the difficulties involved in prolonged dependence on the parents. It is as though a protection against the dread of loss of love, if we can feel that we ourselves are unique beings, individuals, and do not have to fear that one child can without any ado take the place of another in the love of their mother. Everyone who has to do with children knows how they may develop all sorts of 'antics', for fear of being passed over unnoticed. With the recognition of a child's uniqueness we can set its fears at rest, and free it from the desperate need of attracting notice.

We may say generally that about the third or fourth year —at the time, that is, when the mutual tendencies towards detachment are most active in both mother and child—the mother should tender her recognition of the child's individuality as a sort of *parting present on passing out of the phase of early, comparatively unindividualized, childhood.* The reinforcement of individuality is not only a means of reassurance; it is also *a compensation for the long postponement of maturity.* It is the substitute for the lacking independence, and the acknowledgment of the fact that in prolonged childhood the interests of mother and child may diverge widely—may indeed be diametrically opposed. Moreover, this attitude towards the child's individuality holds also a compensation for the mother. The child learns, in time, to see its mother too as an individual being, and so becomes able also to give up its first primitive, egotistic, form of love towards her, i.e. to pay regard to her individual interests. In this manner both mother and child regain something of that instinctual happiness which systematic education took from them.

In conclusion, a few words as to the relation between education and civilization. The study of various peoples shows that there can hardly be any method of education which is not practicable. From the greatest imaginable freedom to the most cruel tyranny, everything has been practised, and the children have borne it. *It is only the particular civilizations themselves that cannot tolerate a deviant system of education.* There is no absolute pedagogy, no absolute mental hygiene. Changes in a civilization must be underpinned by corresponding educational measures, if they are to last. It follows conversely, that reforms in education necessarily bring about a change in the civilization, *even when that was not the conscious intention.* For every improvement affects the whole of the given situation. Hence pedagogics is the most revolutionary of all sciences. Perhaps the inconspicuous 'improvements' in methods of education are the prime mover in cultural evolution, for every educational system has its defects and tends towards change.[1]

---

[1] Could there be a completely perfect system of education (within a given civilization), a complete 'conditioning' (as adumbrated in Huxley's *Brave New World*) to a fixed milieu, the world would have to stand still—as indeed it has done for centuries in China or India, although the coolies and pariahs fared no better than other oppressed classes of the earth.

INDEX

Abraham, Karl, 36, 54
Abreaction, 121
Aggressiveness, 69
Anger, and loving, 99-100
    and projection, 105
Anthropomorphism, 94
Atkinson, 61
Attitude, defensive, to children, 8
Automatisms, 117-18

Balzac, H. de, 29
Birth, curiosity about, 52ff

Caresses, 42-3, 48
Castration anxiety, see Penis anxiety
    complex, 69ff
Censor, see Repression
Childishness, 50
Christianity, 4
Civilization, and education, 145
Cleanliness training, 22ff, 32
Coitus, observation of, 44-6
Commands, attitude to, 112-13, 121-23
Conscience, 113-14, 121
Curiosity, sexual, 51

Dangers, attitude to, 138
Displacement, 92

Educability, of children, 18-19
Education, aims of, 13-14
    demands of, 19

Ego, splitting of, 113-17
Emigration, mental, 110-11, 142
Eskimos, 16-17
'Everything allowed', 16

Father, relation to, 109-10
Fear, of loss of love, 143-44
    of women, 80-1
Feelings, and education, 30
    and science, 2
Ferenczi, S., 65, 116, 125, 142
Fighting, 45
Freud, S., 2, 3, 4, 5, 44, 52, 61, 64, 70, 76, 113, 116, 143

Genital erotism, 33-4, 43, 65
Genitals, female, 80-1
Gratifications, 101, 119-20
Grown-ups, comparison with, 66-7
Guilt, 48-9, 73-4

'Habits, bad', 21
Habituation, 14
Heredity, 2
Hermann, 142
Honesty, need of, 136-37
Hygiene, 133

Identification, 24-5, 92ff
    with parents, 107ff
Incest, 61
Indians, American, 16, 17, 112
Individuality, 143-44
Initiation rites, see Puberty

INDEX

Innocence, pseudo-, 47
Instincts, 11, 19ff
  diversion of, 119
  flexibility of, 31

Jealousy, of siblings, 53-4, 60
  unconscious, 6
Jokes, 5

King, slaying the, 70-1
Kiss, 42

Lang, Andrew, 61
Love, beginnings of, 30
  fear of loss of, 143-44
  and hate, in children, 39-40, 48, 62
Loving, and identification, 99-101

Married life, child's idea of, 42
Masculine women, 89
Masturbation, 33-4, 43-4, 49, 65ff
  excessive, 77-8
  female, 83, 88
  phantasies, 44, 70, 74, 77-8, 88
  place of, 74-5, 79
  and self-love, 106
Memory, of childhood, 3-4
Mental life, in childhood, richness of, 3-4
Mexico, 16
Mistakes, admission of, 125
Morality, 12-13
Mother, relation to, in girls, 85-6, 89-90
Mother-child relationship, 6

Nakedness, 33
Narcissism, 64ff, 95, 103-4, 126

Neurosis, predisposition and environment in, 129

Obedience, 113
Œdipus complex, 34ff
  legend, 61
Omnipotence, parental, 125
Opposite, doing the, 112
Oral erotism, 27, 28, 29, 101

Parents, love of and identification with, 108ff
Pedagogics and psycho-analysis, 11-12
Penis, anxiety, 68-9, 78, 80
  child's view of, 59-60
  envy, 70-1; in girls, 81-2
Petting, 78
Phantasies, masturbation, *see* Masturbation
Play, and identification, 96-7
Pleasure-principle, 20
Primitives, education among, 15-17, 18, 61
Projection, 103, 105, 116
Puberty ceremonies, 15, 142
  mutilation at, 72

Rasmussen, 17, 36, 54, 115
Remembrance, *see* Memory
Renunciation, 19-22
Repression, 2-3, 4, 7-8, 24, 31, 92, 116
  and culture, 18, 74
Retention of faeces, 22-3

Sadism, 45
Satisfaction, egotistic and social, 28
  of instincts, 19-20
  substitute, 21-2, 26

INDEX

Self, relation with, 102-3
Self-love, *see* Narcissism
Self-preservation, instinct of, 69
Sexuality, childhood, 4-5, 33ff
Spoiling, 78
Stern, W. and C., 7
'Stork' myth, 52
Sublimation, 26, 75, 92
    overdone, 76
Sucking, 100-2
Super-ego, 113-14, 116

Thumb-sucking, 21, 26-7

Toys, *see* Play
Trauma, 2, 129

Understanding, and identification, 124
Urban life, children and, 132-33
Urination, and childhood sexuality, 46-7

Vanity, feminine, 83

Women, fear of, *see* Fear
Words, tabooed, 6-7